D0263032

Is God to Blame?

the problem of evil revisited

GERARD J. HUGHES

VERITAS

First published 2007 by
Veritas Publications
7/8 Lower Abbey Street
Dublin 1
Ireland
Email publications@veritas.ie
Website www.veritas.ie

ISBN 978 1 84730 029 4

Copyright © Gerard J. Hughes, 2007

10 9 8 7 6 5 4 3 2 1

The material in this publication is protected by copyright law. Except as may be
permitted by law, no part of the material may be reproduced (including by storage in
a retrieval system) or transmitted in any form or by any means, adapted, rented or lent
without the written permission of the copyright owners. Applications for permissions
should be addressed to the publisher.

A catalogue record for this book
is available from the British Library.

The Scripture quotations contained herein are from the *New Revised Standard Version
Bible*, copyright © 1989 by the Division of Christian Education of the National
Council of the Churches of Christ in the U.S.A., and are used with permission. All
rights reserved.

Printed in the Republic of Ireland
by Betaprint Dublin

Veritas books are printed on paper made from the wood pulp of managed forests. For
every tree felled, at least one tree is planted, thereby renewing natural resources.

CONTENTS

ACKNOWLEDGEMENTS

I would like to thank Victoria Bennett, Maria Cockerill and Deirdre Johnson for helping me to make the style and content more readily accessible to people who are interested, are not necessarily specialists in philosophy or theology, and have ordinary busy lives to lead. My Jesuit colleagues here at Campion Hall, Philip Endean and Nicholas King, offered many important suggestions, both erudite and editorial, which I have tried to take into account. I am also most grateful to the Jesuit community at Centre Sèvres in Paris for providing a most welcoming and delightful environment for my study leave last autumn, during which this book was written.

The reader is asked not to blame any of the above for the remaining shortcomings of this book. It is unfortunately true that most writers on this topic are unlikely to provide a solution, and are therefore all too aware of being themselves part of The Problem.

INTRODUCTION

One way or another, we are all familiar with suffering and misfortune. Not a day passes without there being news of whole populations suffering from starvation and disease, from systematic rape and wanton massacre. We hear of the hopelessness of poverty and illiteracy and the desperation of the displaced. For some of us, too, tragedy strikes in an immediately personal way – the death of a parent or other loved one. Less dramatically, but often no more easily borne, there are the debilitating effects of unemployment, of broken relationships, of degenerative illness. Maybe it is the very immediacy of personal tragedy which makes us look insistently for someone to blame – the doctors, the police, the government, anyone we can find on whom to release our anger and bitterness and sense of total loss. Perhaps it is the immediacy of personal tragedy which most readily prompts people to blame God; how could God do this to me, how could he allow my innocent child to die, let my spouse go off with someone else leaving me bereft and on my own, not care that I have been unemployed for more than two years? But when we look beyond ourselves and reflect upon the enormous suffering inflicted by earthquakes, tsunamis, hurricanes, AIDS and the viciousness of our fellow humans, it is hard to avoid asking how this can possibly be God's world? Or, if it is, what kind of God must there be who creates a world like this? Perhaps there is no ultimate meaning to our lives. Maybe we must just make the best of what we have, in the realisation that we are no more than a by-product of cosmic forces which are as impersonal as they are blind?

Is God to Blame?

Few if any of us will never have felt the force of such questions and the inadequacy of whatever answers we might have produced. It is not just that our responses are often emotionally inadequate; it is that we do not seem even to be able to think of an explanation which would satisfy us intellectually either. The 'explanations' are so often glib, worse than no explanation at all. This book is prompted by two basic concerns: the first is to show that belief in a good God even in the face of suffering and misfortunes can still be characterised by intellectual honesty and integrity; and the second is the need to discover what can, and perhaps more immediately what cannot, be said in answer to the questions with which all of us will at some time or other be beset.

Despite the way in which nostalgic reference is sometimes made to the Ages of Faith, as though religious belief in some golden age was quite unproblematic, I do not think there ever was an age in which the existence of God was simply unquestioned. Even in the eleventh century St Anselm is moved to confront the person who 'says in his heart that there is no God', and to try to produce reasoned arguments against that view. In the thirteenth century St Thomas Aquinas is well known for his insistence that faith requires reason. The believer will of course have to accept some truths simply on God's authority; but the believer will not be justified in accepting that authority unless in the first place there are good reasons to believe that there exists a God who does provide such revelation. And of course it is just obvious that reason is an essential tool in trying to grasp the meaning of what God has revealed, and to integrate that knowledge with everything else we might claim to know.

Since the Enlightenment the charge often brought against religious belief is precisely that there are no really convincing grounds for believing that there is a God at all. The extent of 'meaningless' suffering and misfortune in our world is alleged to hammer the last nail into the coffin of justifiable religious belief.

That is why the honesty and integrity of religious belief depends (among other things, of course) upon refuting the alleged

6

Introduction

incompatibility between the existence of a good God and the tragedies of our sorry world. It is not enough for the believer to claim that since there clearly is a God, there is no real need to take the Enlightenment challenge seriously. Confronted with the near meaninglessness of tragedy, whether personal or cosmic, the religious believer is faced with a most uncomfortable dilemma: either religious belief in an infinitely good God must simply be abandoned as incompatible with any honest attempt to face up to the ills of our world; or else The Problem must simply be ignored, left somewhere at the back of one's mind slowly corroding the picture of God that we have.

So in the first part of this book, I have one very positive aim. I hope to give good reasons for claiming that even the worst features of our world do not provide good grounds for denying that our world is the loving expression of a good God. Even if we can say nothing more positive, at least to establish that will dispel the most acute versions of the challenge. I shall not be undertaking the much larger task of proving that there is a God and that God is loving and omnipotent. To do that would require another book entirely. But it is essential to defeat the argument which tries to establish that it simply *cannot* be reasonable to believe in a good God whose providence governs our world.

The second part of the book tries to prove something quite different. Even if I have successfully shown that a belief in the providence of a good God is not an irrational and untenable belief, that is a very long way from showing in detail how every suffering or misfortune in our world does in the end work out for the best. It seems to me that the history of attempts to provide detailed answers of that kind to questions such as, 'How can God permit this?' shows that such attempts are apt to do much more harm than good. The proposed justifications for God's actions lack clarity or conviction, or both, and proposing them can be damaging. To substantiate this claim I propose to examine the various kinds of explanation for the sufferings in the world which the biblical writers, whether Jewish or

Christian, have tried to offer, and to show what I take to be their weaknesses. In particular, I shall consider what, from a Christian point of view, seemed to be one of the most intractably terrible events – the death of Jesus – and look at the attempts they made to explain what God was doing in allowing his Son to be treated in such a way. I shall argue that these explanations, too, mostly do more harm than good, and that no explanations are better than such bad ones. I shall make no attempt to answer desperately pressing questions such as, 'Why did God let my child die?' Of course, *some* kind of answer can usually be given: the child died of meningitis, say, or in a road accident. But it is not at that level that the agonising question is asked. What the bereaved person desperately wants is to find some *meaning* in such a tragedy which will relate it to the goodness of a provident God. I will not attempt to provide such answers because I simply do not believe that we have such answers at our disposal. I shall discuss the arguments of those biblical writers who caution us against looking for detailed explanations.

Does this book, then, offer 'naught for your comfort'?[1] I shall argue that there are indeed good grounds for being comforted, even though we simply cannot satisfy our need for a fuller explanation of how God's providence governs our world. In the final chapter I shall suggest that instead of looking for intellectual solutions to The Problem, we would do better to consider the ways in which the Bible suggests we should respond to suffering – ways which both make good sense and are intellectually honest, even though they are not 'solutions' to The Problem in any traditional sense.

One final note. 'The Problem of Evil' is too deeply rooted as an expression for me to be able to avoid it altogether. But it is not at all

---

1   The phrase is from G.K. Chesterton's 'Ballad of the White Horse':
    I tell you naught for your comfort,
    yea, naught for your desire,
    save that the sky grows darker yet
    and the sea rises higher.

accurate. The difficulty is that 'evil' is intended as a translation of the Latin *malum*. But *malum* in Latin is a very wide term, corresponding more closely to a word like 'bad' in English: it can be used to refer to a headache or a bad cold, as well as to major natural disasters such as a tsunami or an earthquake, none of which would naturally be called 'evils' in English; and even in moral matters it can refer to losing one's temper, which is a bad but hardly an evil thing to do, as well as to moral outrages such as the Holocaust or the massacres in Cambodia under Pol Pot, which really are evil. I shall try to use whatever English word is most natural in the various contexts; and sometimes it will be simplest just to speak of 'The Problem'.

Part I

CHAPTER ONE

'THE PROBLEM OF EVIL'

'The Problem of Evil' has both a natural setting, and a cultural history. Its natural setting is in the context of the great monotheist religions, for it is to them that the challenges can be most forcefully addressed. In the context of the belief that there is just one all-powerful creator God, and that the powerful creator God is also perfectly good and all knowing, it is at once difficult to see how our world can be so overwhelmed by the sufferings we can see all around us. Anyone who has been tragically bereaved might well ask, 'How could God let this happen to me? Could God not have arranged things in a better way? Would that have been too much to ask?' In circumstances of extreme wrong and suffering, such as the situation of the prisoners in the Nazi concentration camps, even pious Jews were driven to ask, 'And where is God now? Why is God silent?' At the limit, the question is no longer just a way of blaming God; it expresses the despair of someone forced to contemplate the terrible possibility that there is no God at all.

In an atheistic context, of course, the situation is quite different. Someone who has been tragically bereaved will want to know what happened and why; the explanation may consist in a medical diagnosis, or in a detailed account of an accident; it may or may not be that the explanation involves someone else being to blame. The unbeliever will of course want to know how it happened, and may well be interested in seeing whether there might be ways of avoiding similar tragedies in future. But the impulse to ask, 'How could this happen to me?' and even the lack of an adequate answer poses no threat at all to their world view. Indeed the unbeliever might well consider it an advantage of their position that such cosmic questions simply do not arise. It is enough to have to cope with tragedy without in addition being forced to raise issues about making sense of one's whole life.

The Roman poet Horace expressed a response to this kind of view with a noble beauty:

> Iustum et tenacem propositi virum
> non civium ardor prava iubentium,
> non vultus instantis tyranni
> mente quatit solida neque Auster
> dux inquieti turbidus Hadriae,
> nec fulminantis magna manus Iovis:
> si fractus illabatur orbis,
> impavidum ferient ruinae.[1]

> *An upright man, of purpose firm —*
> *No citizens, though eager to corrupt,*
> *Nor tyrant's glare demanding he do wrong,*
> *Nor howling South Wind, Adriatic's king,*
> *Nor Jove's hand, hurling thunderbolts*
> *Will ever shake him from his chosen course.*
> *If round him were to fall this shattered world,*
> *Its wreckage would engulf him fearless still.*

There is here no question whatever of blaming God for the disasters which threaten. Jove is mentioned only in a conventional sense. What is important is not why there are such things as corrupt men, or violence in humans and in the destructive power of nature; these are the brute, often enough the brutal, facts of life. What is important

---

1   Horace *Odes*, III, 3, lines 1–8.

is the integrity which can still be preserved despite them all. For those who live up to Horace's ideal even our shattered world does not raise the troubling questions the theist has to face. They do not have to reason why, in that disturbing sense; they have to accept and to live in the world with an incorruptible courage, rather than allow themselves to be undermined by terror and useless complaint.

Again, in cultures which are in some way polytheist, The Problem can be relatively quickly handled, by postulating the existence of a source of disorder fighting with a source of order for control of the world. The early Greek philosopher Empedocles thought of the cosmos as composed of the four unchanging elements, earth, air, fire and water, continually being arranged and dispersed under the power of two personified cosmic forces. Here are two of the fragments we have from him:

> (16) For even as they [Strife and Love] were aforetime,
> so too they shall be; nor ever, methinks, will boundless
> time be emptied of that pair.
> (17) I shall tell thee a twofold tale. At one time it grew
> to be one only out of many; at another, it divided up
> to be many instead of one. There is a double birth of
> perishable things and a double passing away. The
> coming together of all things brings one generation
> into being and destroys it; the other grows up and is
> scattered as things become divided. And these things
> never cease continually changing places, at one time all
> uniting in one through Love, at another each borne in
> different directions by the repulsion of Strife.

Empedocles' principal intention is to explain change, and the processes by which things in the universe come to be and cease to be. He does not primarily aim at solving The Problem of Evil as it confronts a theist, despite the way in which the personification might suggest that there is one good and one bad cosmic force. He probably does not believe that when something in the universe ceases to be something must have gone wrong. He is offering a model to help us to understand the duality and opposition which seems to pervade our universe. Love is not somehow more admirable than Strife, any more than our contemporary terminology is meant to suggest that forces of attraction are better than forces of repulsion in the natural world. This is just a natural fact about how things are, not something which we need to see in moral terms.

But of course, moral explanations too can easily be provided. It is quite possible to try to account for the things which are wrong in our world as well as for everything which is valuable by postulating two equally fundamental beings, one morally good, one morally evil. One would assume that neither of them would have produced the other, for neither would have any reason to do so. On this kind of view, of course, belief in the God on whom everything else depends has simply been abandoned. It is only when someone believes in a single, good, all powerful and all-knowing God that the Problem arises at once with all its force. The fact that there is suffering and misery in the world is as evident to the monotheist believer as it is to the atheist or the polytheist, but their responses are simply not available to the monotheist. An all powerful, all-good, all-knowing God must surely be all-responsible as well; and it is that responsibility for our sufferings, misfortunes and tragedies which seems so hard to square with belief in God's goodness. Yet The Problem simply cannot with any honesty or integrity be simply swept under the carpet. Monotheists are in a serious position because of their very monotheism itself.

Even within its natural monotheist setting, The Problem of Evil has had a varied cultural history. Two main factors can be singled out as crucial to the ways in which The Problem is seen and the kinds of solutions which are proposed.

The first is connected with the various ways in which monotheists think of the goodness of God. In general, of course, believers of all kinds construct their notion of God on the basis of their experience of human persons. We should therefore expect that the ways in which believers have talked about God will have been considerably influenced by the ethics of their various cultures. People do not have, and certainly have not had, just one view of what it is to be an admirable human being. And, since we would not for the most part expect less of God than we would of one another, we humans have had a variety of pictures of what it is for God to be good. Of course most theists would be alert to the danger of conceiving God simply in our own image, and are careful to introduce qualifications to prevent such imaginative images being applied to God too directly. Still, the morality which obliges us is inseparably tied to the kind of beings that we are, and the ways in which we are able to live fulfiled lives together. In theistic terms, God's moral demands upon us are not arbitrarily decided on, but are deeply integrated with the way in which he created us. God would therefore be inconsistent were he to treat us in ways which were contrary to the moral demands we are naturally bound to make on one another. For our part, we could not believe in the goodness of a god whose moral behaviour violated our own moral ideals.

But perhaps it was not always so. Take for instance the qualities of being just and authoritative. It is possible to find in the Islamic, Jewish and Christian traditions expressions which suggest that the authority of God is such that he can simply decide what is to count as just and what is not. His prerogative is absolute and unconstrained. However traditional it might be argued to be, most of our contemporaries would quite rightly find such a picture of God far too close for comfort to recent experiences of untrammelled dictatorship. We would probably not wish to say that God is somehow constrained by moral standards outside himself; but in one way or another we expect God's internal self-constraints to be at least analogous to our own, and, as I have just argued, to be consistent with the needs of the people he has created. Most of us, though indeed perhaps not all, would not be willing to believe in a God whose moral behaviour, or whose moral demands, we occasionally found difficult to comprehend. But to be able to worship and to admire God as good we need to believe that God's moral standards, though they may indeed be higher, are still not discontinuous with our own.

To take an example. We ourselves are far from clear about the precise relationships we might want to have between being forgiving, being merciful, being vengeful and administering just punishments. We are often quite ambivalent about how we think forgiveness should function in our society. Can one forgive only someone who is sorry for the wrong that they did? Should we generously forgive people who are sorry, without punishing them at all? Or would that policy tend to suggest that we were not particularly concerned about the wrong that was done? Perhaps it is important to punish wrongdoers simply as an expression of the importance of openly upholding moral standards? These are very live questions in countries such as South Africa and Northern Ireland. Should people simply draw a line under the past, declare an amnesty, and try to rebuild a new society with no further recrimination, or would such policies wrongly ignore something which the new society itself should still insist upon? Is it easier, or indeed more necessary, to forgive such a person if one knows that such a person was acting in accordance with their own highest ideals?

Again, most – though again not all – of us would be far from accepting the legitimacy of such practices as blood feuds or 'honour' killings. To be avenged would not be one of our moral ideals. Yet even if we would therefore not wish to think of just punishment as revenge or as some kind of 'paying back', since that would be incompatible with forgiveness, we might nevertheless think that at least some public expression of our outrage at a gross violation of our moral standards is required if those standards are to be upheld and inculcated.

I offer those examples simply in the form of questions, since I do not believe that there is anything like a universal consensus among various believers about what the answers might be. My point is that such differences of opinion will be reflected also in our beliefs about God's justice, mercy, punishments and forgiveness. As a result there are wide differences of opinion about whether we can ever, or even sometimes, explain an unwelcome event in our world as being a punishment from God, and so try to lessen some of the impact of The Problem. Many of the misfortunes related in the Jewish Bible are explained in terms of God punishing the people, or individuals, for their infidelity. It is certainly true that many contemporary Christians are willing to justify some of the misfortunes of our own world – the AIDS pandemic would be one example – as God's punishment for immoral conduct, and hence as presenting no problem for the believer in a good God.

The other influence evident in the history of The Problem of Evil within monotheist cultures is the enormous progress in our scientific understanding of the universe. Before the scientific revolutions in the seventeenth century, in much of the Christian, Jewish and Muslim world there was no plausible alternative to the view that God is the ultimate explanation of the universe as we know it. If such a belief in God is not seriously called into question, then it is easy to assume that The Problem of Evil must somehow have a solution, even if that solution is not at all evident to us. Believers may admit to inadequate knowledge; they may prefer some approaches to others on moral grounds; but in the last analysis The Problem is known not to be fatal. Christians, for example, can honestly continue in their faith even in the face of such disasters as the death of the Messiah, as could Jews in their most cherished beliefs after the destruction of the Temple in 70CE. I shall argue that this sense of ultimate security was by no means an unmixed blessing, in that it often encouraged people to be content with over-rapid sketches of possible solutions. But in any event, when the development of science and the attitudes of the Enlightenment generally began to suggest that after all there may not be any good reasons for belief in God, and that such belief may perhaps not be necessary in order to make sense of the universe, The Problem began to assume much more serious proportions. The difference can be easily illustrated.

Medieval authors often speak quite calmly about the way in which dark parts of a picture can bring out the beauty of the colours. Using this comparison they can readily suggest that the punishment of people in hell serves to exhibit the justice of God.

Thus St Augustine can say:

> To thee there is no such thing as evil, and even in thy whole creation taken as a whole, there is not; because there is nothing from beyond it that can burst in and destroy the order which thou hast appointed for it. But in the parts of creation, some things, because they do not harmonise with others, are considered evil. Yet those same things harmonise with others and are good, and in themselves are good. And all these things which do not harmonise with each other still harmonise with the inferior part of creation which we call the earth, having its own cloudy and windy sky of like nature with itself. Far be it from me, then, to say, 'These things should not be'. For if I could see nothing but these, I should indeed desire something better – but still I ought to praise thee, if only for these created things. But seeing also that in heaven all thy angels praise thee, O God, praise thee in the heights, 'and all thy hosts, sun and moon, all stars and light, the heavens of heavens, and the waters that are above the heavens', praise thy name – seeing this, I say, I no longer desire a better world, because my thought ranged over all, and with a sounder judgment I reflected that the things above were better than those below, yet that all creation together was better than the higher things alone.[2]

Aquinas writes in similar vein at the very beginning of his *Summa Theologiae* when replying to someone who says that there cannot be a God, for if there were, there would be no evil:

---

2 Augustine, *Confessions* VII, xiii, 19.

In response to the first objection, then, I repeat what Augustine says; that since God is entirely good, He would permit evil to exist in His works only if He were so good and omnipotent that He might bring forth good even from the evil. It therefore pertains to the infinite goodness of God that he permits evil to exist and from this brings forth good.[3]

And he elaborates the same idea somewhat further on when speaking about God's providence:

There is a difference between someone who has to look after just one thing, and someone who has to look after absolutely everything: the first will do his best to ensure that the thing he is in charge of has no defect in it at all; but the person who is in charge of everything can permit a defect in an individual thing so as not to obstruct the good of the whole. That natural things are subject to decay and corruption is indeed against their individual natures, but accords with the purpose of nature in general, in so far as a defect in one is to the benefit of another or even of everything else. For one thing to die is for another to come to be, to preserve the species. Since God's providence extends to all that is, it allows some defects in individual things so as not to obstruct the good of the whole. There would be no lion alive unless other animals were killed, nor would there be the endurance of the martyrs were there no tyrants to persecute them.[4]

3 Aquinas, *Summa Theologiae* I, 2, 3, reply to 1st objection.
4 Aquinas, ibid., I, 22, reply to 2nd objection.

Is God to Blame?

What is so striking about these passages is the complete confidence with which the argument is stated. The confidence derives from the fact that Aquinas believes that he has already shown that there must exist a God, and that he has done so beyond any doubt. In the light of that, it simply has to be the case that the sorrows and misfortunes of our world are part of God's plan, and hence good in that larger perspective, even though the detail can be violent, bloody and threatening to dumb animals as well as heroic martyrs. Augustine and Aquinas had no urgent need to ensure that The Problem really could be dealt with in detail. Contrast with these two writers the following passage from David Hume:

> It must be allowed that, if a very limited intelligence, whom we shall suppose utterly unacquainted with the universe, were assured that it were the production of a very good, wise, and powerful Being, however finite, he would, from his conjectures, form *beforehand* a different notion of it from what we find it to be by experience; nor would he ever imagine merely from these attributes of the cause of which he is informed, that the effect could be so full of vice and misery and disorder, as it appears in this life ... But supposing, which is the real case with regard to man, that this creature is not antecedently convinced of a supreme intelligence, benevolent and powerful, but is left to gather such a belief from the appearances of things – this entirely alters the case, nor will he ever find reason for such a conclusion.[5]

Post-enlightenment theists cannot simply 'be assured' that God has it all under control. That confident medieval solution is no longer readily acceptable because the existence of God is now not the only

5   *Dialogues concerning Natural Religion*, XI.

hypothesis on offer when it comes to explaining the existence of the universe. Even in the minds of believers it has to compete with a variety of other proposed explanations offered by the physical sciences, and must show that it is as rigorously argued and as credible as they are. To do that, *all* the evidence needs to be considered; which surely must include the counter-evidence that there is so much pain, misfortune, disaster and brutality in the world as we know it. Hume's claim is that on the basis of the evidence nobody could reasonably conclude that there is an all-powerful benevolent supreme intelligence. He refuses to accept that The Problem can be reasonably dealt with by quiet assurances.

Hume has accurately diagnosed the spirit of his, and our, times. Widespread doubts about the existence of God are now an integral part of a culture where there is no escape from the scale of human suffering in our world, suffering inflicted by the brutality of other humans, and by the blind forces of an uncontrolled nature. We can do one another such terrible damage, by rejection, by abuse, by exclusion, by psychological and physical violence; we can look on helplessly as floods and earthquakes and epidemics destroy people's entire world. Every day we can see the absolute misery of wrecked and hopeless lives, the lives of people to whom the calm thoughts of Augustine or Aquinas, even were they true, would seem utterly inadequate, since they apparently suggest that their sufferings, like the shadows in the picture, are enhancements to the world as a whole. Some much more sustained argument is required, therefore, which does not presuppose the existence of God but nevertheless is sufficient at least to question Hume's sceptical conclusion.

No book, no philosophical or theological discussion, is remotely capable of making much impact on global misery, and this book has no such ambitions. How to assuage suffering is not at all the same problem as The Problem of Evil, which is directed at understanding rather than comforting. My targets are confusions rather than sufferings; not that there cannot be any connection between the two, but it is at best indirect.

Is God to Blame?

There are two strategies for attacking The Problem. The first might be called the ambitious strategy: The Problem is to be solved, so the aim must be to show exactly how each instance of suffering and so on can be explained in a way which is entirely compatible with the goodness of God. On this approach, one would try to show how it is that in the long run things will work out for the best; or else that all suffering is duly deserved; or else that it can be understood in terms of one or other of the traditional categories such as redemptive suffering or sacrifice. In short, the aim would be to provide a theodicy – an account of how God is justified in all his actions, and how it is that each individual's suffering will be for the best. The shadows genuinely contribute to the beauty of the picture, and we can show how they do so.

I shall not attempt to adopt this strategy. This is not because I do not believe that God is justified in what he does. Any believer must surely believe that. My reason for not adopting the ambitious strategy is not that it must be utterly flawed in principle and not just in detail. Augustine and Aquinas must surely be right at least to this extent, that God's creation must be good overall. Where it seems to me that they are mistaken is in suggesting that it is good in part *because of* rather than *despite* the bad things it contains. Their approach leads one to expect detailed 'solutions' which for a variety of reasons I believe to be quite unconvincing. The complexities of our world are such as to make so ambitious a project simply beyond reach. Worse, I shall argue that attempts to provide a theodicy – a justification of God's actions – in this detailed way, claiming that everything contributes to the glory of the whole, is much more likely to do damage. Such 'explanations' are at best unhelpful, and at worst misleading or downright false.

I shall therefore adopt a much less ambitious plan. The anti-theist claims to have shown that it is impossible or at any rate highly unlikely that a good God could have created a universe like ours. I intend to argue that they have not succeeded establishing either version of that conclusion. This might at first sight seem a rather disappointing approach. To show that for all we know The Problem of Evil is only an apparent problem is cold comfort indeed. But this seemingly minimalist result is much more important than it at first sight appears. For if it can be shown that The Problem of Evil need not be fatal to theism, we shall have established the first and crucial point, that it is possible to be an intellectually honest believer in God who is good. One does not have to sweep The Problem under the rug, a practice which is unfortunately as frequent as it is corrosive to religious faith. This is not to say that if this unambitious project succeeds we shall find that the difficulties in coping with the evils in our world will have disappeared. They obviously will do no such thing. The problems of living with and responding to the manifold sufferings of human beings have to be coped with by whatever means, practical and psychological, we can devise. But at least we will know that they need not be complicated by the nagging suspicion that if we cannot provide a complete explanation our faith must be rendered less secure and our lives fundamentally dishonest.

CHAPTER TWO

BLAMING GOD?

To believe in a good God is not simply to believe that God is a good thing, in the way in which to enjoy a pleasant meal or to be able to support one's family are good things. To believe in a good God is to trust in a God whom we believe to be worthy of worship, and morally admirable in a way that we can recognise even if we cannot fully comprehend. If The Problem of Evil threatens this view of God, it must get its force from the suggestion that God is somehow morally substandard in creating as he has; in other words, that it is reasonable to blame God for what God has done (or failed to do). Indeed it is precisely in these words that The Problem very often is expressed. Particularly when the suffering is one's own, or has had devastating effects on those one loves or for whom one works, a natural response is to want to blame God – for a bereavement, a ruined life or the multiple agonies of the refugee camp. For the believer, it may simply not seem enough just to blame one's fellow humans – Nazis, abusive parents, corrupt politicians – nor simply to resign oneself to the awesome power of nature: the believer might be strongly inclined to insist that responsibility can stop only at the highest point. Ultimately it is the creator who is responsible and must be called to account. The instinct to blame God is a completely understandable consequence of an unreserved belief in God's sovereignty, and is a very natural response to feeling betrayed by a God who is love.

As I have said, the full counter-argument would require us to show exactly how everything that God has done is justified; but this ambitious project is beyond our capabilities. Instead, I shall pursue the modest aim of undermining the arguments which seek to show that we are justified in blaming God. If you like, it is a version of the presumption of innocence: God must in all justice be held innocent unless it can be shown that God is blameworthy. So the case to be made is that this has not been shown beyond any reasonable doubt. Of course this would not show that a good God exists; it would show only that the woes of our world do not rule that out.

First, then, we must try to set out the conditions to be met in order to be justified in blaming anyone. We can set these out quite generally, relying on the general framework of our ordinary moral judgements. If what was said above is true, we have no better standards against which to measure God's conduct than those which we would use to assess our own.

So, when are we justified in blaming someone for something? In this context we are not talking of 'blame' in the sense in which we might blame the bad summer for the poor harvest, or dry rot for the fact that the beams in the ceiling have become unsafe. 'Blame' in those cases is used in a weaker sense which requires simply that we establish the relevant connection between the alleged cause and the supposed undesirable effect. In contrast, blaming someone morally requires that the person can be considered as a moral agent. So what are the conditions which have to be met if we are to blame a moral agent? I suggest that they are as follows:

A person can be blamed for something provided each of the following conditions is met:
i) The action done is bad all things considered
ii) The person performed that action
iii) The person knew what they were doing and how things would turn out
iv) The person could have done better
v) The person knew that they could have done better.[1]

---

1   The first three conditions are slightly oversimplified in the interests of clarity. Strictly speaking they would have to be modified to deal with the fact that we can blame someone for states of affairs that they brought about, as well as for their actions.

In the first condition, 'bad all things considered' is a crucial but far from clear phrase. We do, of course, have a general idea of what is meant. We often have to take medicines which have undesirable side effects; but those need not make taking that drug bad all things considered. In complex cases, we frequently have to make overall assessments which are very complex indeed, as we try to balance the pros and cons. Which of these applicants should be given the job? Should we employ skilled people from undeveloped countries who come here for a better life and to support their relatives at home? At what point should we say to someone that a further surgical operation would do no good? It would be wonderful if there were clear methods for reaching reliable conclusions about such problems every time. I do not for one moment believe that there are, although to defend that statement would involve a long excursion into ethical theory which would be quite beyond the scope of this book. I can hope only that when we come to applying this requirement in the context of our present argument, we can do it without making any indefensible assumptions. It is often not too difficult to agree on which are the relevant considerations in such cases; but how they balance out in this or that instance is, in the end, not something we can usually expect to calculate exactly.

The second condition, 'being the cause', is also stated in very general terms. So, consider a road accident, in which a car being driven round a corner at 25 miles an hour by a man who has had one drink that evening skidded on the icy surface and crashed into a tree, killing the passenger. What was the cause of the death? The driver (a philosopher!) might try to argue that the cause was the oxygen in the atmosphere, without which the car could not have run at all. And to be sure, the oxygen in the atmosphere did have a causal influence on what happened. Was it therefore *the cause* of what happened? The very idea may at first sound absurd: but would it be so absurd to suggest that, since there would be no wrong actions at all did God not create the world, then God must be the cause of all those actions? Some people have indeed argued just that: the First Cause

(God) must cause everything, and hence be responsible for everything. In reasonable practice, however, to establish 'the cause of death' is not just a matter of physics, medicine and meteorology. Nor can it be settled simply by saying things like, 'If such and such had not been the case, the person would never have died'. In assigning responsibility, we try to isolate the *relevant* feature(s) from the other factors present at the time. In practice we look for a variety of different things according to the context: sometimes we focus on what is unusual or unexpected, sometimes on what was incompetent or careless. So was the cause of death the ice, the speed, the drink, carelessness? Or was there no legally relevant cause and all we can say is that it was just an accident? Coroners have to exercise judgement – there is no automatic formula for getting it right. (And, when all else fails, the insurance company will tell us that it was an act of God!)

Finally, the last two conditions as here expressed take no account of someone being negligently ignorant. However, when we come to apply all these conditions to God we presumably do not need to consider whether God might have been culpably negligent, so for our purposes the final two conditions can be simpler than they would otherwise have been.

It is important to note that *all five* of these conditions must be satisfied if someone is to be justifiably blamed. If the first is not satisfied, the issue of blaming cannot even arise: one cannot blame someone for something which is overall good. Nor can one blame someone for something they did not do; nor if they had no reason to know of the damage they were bringing about; nor if at the time there was nothing better that they could have done and should have realised they could have done. Failure to satisfy even one of the conditions exonerates the person completely.

The Problem of Evil in effect suggests that when we try to apply the above tests to God, God may indeed satisfy each of them, and hence turn out to be blameworthy. As applied to God the creator, the tests might look like this:

Is God to Blame?

i)   The world is a bad world all things considered
ii)   God created the world
iii)   God knew how the world would work out
iv)   God could have created a better world than this
v)   God knew he could have created a better world than this.

These are the conditions which must be satisfied if we are to be justified in blaming God for our universe. Isn't it obvious, the prosecution case will go, that the world is overall a tragic place, even if we comfortable well-off Westerners can manage not to look at the rest of it too closely? Again, no theist can deny that if there is a God it is God who brought this tragic world into being. God must surely have known what he was doing. And is any theist going to deny that God could do anything he chooses? Are we really expected to believe that this is the best God can do? If we were promised a world created by a good God, we would certainly have expected something a great deal better than this! Or did God not see what was coming? But of course he did. Surely, then, guilty as charged?

The minimalist strategy I outlined above depends upon undermining this case, since if that case is successfully argued then belief in a good God cannot be honestly held. To undermine the case, what has to be shown is that at least one of the conditions for blaming God has not been successfully proved. In fact, I shall argue that at least two of them, i) and iv), are highly dubious. Plainly, if iv) cannot be established, then neither can v); if a better world was not possible, God could not have known that it was possible. Clearly, then, a large part of the argument will depend on what we make of i) and iv). But it has also been argued that in important ways iii) is not true in the relevant way, and this will have to be looked at as well. In the next chapter, I shall start by arguing that i) has not been shown to be true.

CHAPTER THREE

A BAD WORLD?

It would seem very easy to give a list of the kinds of things or events or states of affairs that the world would be better without. Some examples: a death, the desperate straits of so many of the poor in Africa, terrorism, genetic handicap, the pollution of the environment, malicious gossip, disease, violence, racism. Other items might be more controversial – the extinction of the dinosaurs and the dodo, genetic manipulation, globalisation. What is not in the least controversial is that the world contains many undesirable features. The question is whether the cumulative effect of these features is to render the world a bad place overall.

Some of the items on the list clearly are cases where something has gone wrong – genetic handicap or those illnesses which consist in some physical malfunction. Other things, such as earthquakes or floods, are thought to be bad not exactly because something has gone wrong, but because of the way in which they diminish human welfare in one way or another. But human welfare itself is not at all a simple notion. The utilitarian tradition in moral philosophy has taken 'pain' almost as a synonym for *malum*, just as 'pleasure' has been taken as the equivalent of *bonum*, and interpreted human well-being in terms of the predominance of pleasure over pain. It has to be said that, despite the acid comments of some of their critics, the early utilitarians Jeremy Bentham and John Stuart Mill understood neither of these two terms in a simplistic way. Bentham reminds us that pleasures can derive from such different sources as our physical constitution, religion, aesthetics and our human relationships. Pains, too, can be similarly diverse. Pain can accompany physical damage to our bodies; we can suffer emotional hurt of various kinds; we can feel jealous, abandoned, inadequate; people can long for opportunities to educate themselves, and feel deprived and cheated if those opportunities cannot be found; yet anger can be constructive as well as destructive. We may therefore conveniently take the question whether pain is a bad thing as giving us a useful clue to how we might assess the goodness or badness of the world more generally. Is the existence of pain, then, a bad thing overall from the point of view of our human welfare?

Obviously, physical pain is a built-in response of our bodies to some threat to our overall welfare, a warning system which in general is much to our advantage. In these instances, when the need has been dealt with, the pain disappears – as with hunger, for instance, or the healing of a wound; in others, once the discomfort has pointed to the need, the discomfort itself will tend to disappear, its job done. We can, for instance, eventually find that we have shut out intrusive noises without even trying. But it is not always the case that pain is helpful. We sometimes suffer pain from conditions which we can do nothing to ameliorate – some terminal cancers for instance. The difficulty is that the mechanism which is in general terms of great advantage to us is not good at discriminating between threats which can be countered and those which cannot.

Something similar can be said about psychological pain. Feelings of anger, hurt and loneliness can often prompt us to repair some of the human relationships on which our personal welfare depends. Even pains deriving from an irreparable loss – say, a young mother losing her husband in a tragic accident – point to a deep need to grieve; but once that need has been truly met, the person can move on. On the other hand, there are also pains arising in the course of some psychological illnesses which may express damage that cannot readily, or cannot reliably, be cured at all.

Two questions arise therefore: firstly, whether or not our ability to feel pain is overall a good thing; and secondly, whether or not some more discriminating warning system would have been better? The second of these we may postpone until we consider the fourth condition, whether God could have done better than he did in creating the world. But how are we to respond to the first? I suppose I have an intuitive sense that I am much better off with the capacities I now have to feel physical and emotional pain than I would be if one or other of those capacities were simply to be taken away. This can happen in some forms of leprosy, with the result that the sufferers are much more at risk since they can suffer from burns or wounds without noticing. For what it is worth, then, it seems to me that the ability to feel pain is not a bad thing overall; and it might be pointed out on general evolutionary grounds that our present pain/pleasure systems must have conferred some overall advantage. As with so many issues in this area, I do not think there is any possibility of a rigorous proof, but I think the evidence is in favour of the systems which we have.

Similar considerations apply to death. When do we think someone's death is a bad thing? That will depend on wider considerations concerning that individual's welfare and how their death fits into the desire each of us has to live a fulfiled life, as well as on the extent to which other people have come to depend on that person's talents and support. Think, for example, of the death of an elderly person who had the sole care for a severely handicapped son. What might in some ways have been a blessed release for her is also something she would not have wanted for her son's sake. An apparently healthy baby dying suddenly and inexplicably seems such a tragic event, precisely because we think of children as full of hope, with the whole of their lives before them, lives which could have been fulfiled in so many ways. Cot deaths are an extreme case of the way we respond to many other deaths in which people are cut down in their prime. But not all deaths strike us in this way; of some we might say that the person had had a really happy life, and their death was a natural and fitting end to that life. We react similarly to our increased technological ability to postpone death: in some cases with great gratitude, since the person has so much more to live for and look forward to; in other cases with much more hesitation. Despite what is so often said, we do not believe that life is a value which overrides all others. This might suggest that, all things considered, it is not clearly established that our being subject to death is necessarily a bad thing, when everything is taken into account. And of course there is the brute fact that if people, and indeed organisms generally, did not die, we would either have an insupportably overpopulated world, or else a world in which the population was totally fixed over time. Neither alternative seems at all attractive.

Feeling physical or psychological pain is often a first indication of the many other things which are wrong with our world, beset as so many of us are with disease, hunger, lack of basic human comforts, deprived of any chance of an education. These are surely unalloyed misfortunes. Natural events, such as earthquakes, tsunamis, hurricanes and volcanic eruptions, are seen as bad not in themselves, but in the effects that they can have on human welfare.

Everything I have so far said has taken it for granted that whether overall this is a bad world or not has to be judged from our human point of view: is this a world in which humans can lead fulfiled lives? Our preoccupation with human welfare is of course entirely understandable. Yet we often exhibit a willingness to expand our horizons, and to concede that ours is perhaps not the only legitimate viewpoint from which to estimate the overall value of our world. Of course we believe that it is wrong to cause animals needless pain or neglect, because their welfare, too, is value in its own right. On the other hand many, though certainly not all, of us are willing to use animals in a way which we would never dream of using one another. Animal welfare is commonly valued less than our own. And it is noteworthy as well as entirely understandable that when people point to processes such as global warming they may well point out the initial impact on animal populations; but in the last analysis the ultimate threat is that the human race in the last extremity could become extinct. The assumption is that this would be terrible indeed.

Less is said about other extinct animals in that extremity. Do we consider it a terrible feature of our world that the dinosaurs and the dodo have become extinct? There is, of course, a kind of romantic sympathy for those mighty animals, about which we are only gradually becoming informed. But is it a tragedy that they are no more? My sense is that we think of it as simply a historical accident whose cause is uncertain; we tend to say that, after all, these things do happen. But is it not much stranger that we seem to have so little sympathy for Neanderthal man, another blind alley in the evolutionary path, despite the fact that they are closer to ourselves than any dinosaur?

Our tendency to concentrate, even if not quite exclusively, on human welfare is a special case of a more general problem in deciding what is to count as a bad thing overall. For consider a lioness catching a gazelle: is that a bad thing – part of The Problem as it were – or not? From the point of view of the lioness and her cubs, the successful hunt is clearly a good thing. Perhaps from the point of view of that gazelle, it is a bad thing; but it should probably be seen as a good thing from the point of view of the herd of gazelles, since it tends to preserve the kind of balance which prevents over-population and helps to ensure adequate food supplies for the survivors. And indeed, from a general point of view, it would obviously not be a good thing if animals or plants did not tend towards a natural death. However, might it not still be said that the worst feature of so many of the living things on our planet, including us humans, is the way in which they have to support themselves by preying on other organisms? And a further uncomfortable point: to the extent that we are willing to conduct our lives at the expense of individuals in other species – be they trees or sheep – can we then so easily claim that it is a bad thing overall if other species – viruses, bacteria, parasites, other animals – treat us similarly? Should the easy assumption that we are top of the tree be simply taken for granted?

It is fashionable to appeal to the 'ecological balance' – the pattern of behaviour between species which might best ensure their common survival – as the test for the point of view from which all these matters should be judged. But the mere fact, if it is a fact, that the species in our planet can be balanced in this way does not show that a world in which such mutual destruction can balance out is a good world overall, let alone the best world that might have been produced. Similarly, a theist might try to argue that, rather than taking the point of view of some particular species – which would in practice amount to taking ourselves as of central importance – one should take God's point of view, from which the balance of all the species in creation is clearly good overall. But this argument is no better, albeit no worse, than the argument based on an ecological balance. In both cases, we are invited, as it were, to take what has been called the 'View from Nowhere' in the interests of impartiality. The difficulty with this suggestion is that to judge from nowhere in particular is to lack any of the interests in terms of which any judgement could be made; and since we are not able to be sure of seeing things from God's point of view, to try to look at things from that point of view is in practice pretty much equivalent to looking at them from Nowhere. The conclusion therefore must be that we are not in a position to say that the world is good overall prior to establishing that it is the creation of a good God. And to the extent that the evidence suggests that it is not good overall, then the possibility of establishing that there is a good God is to that extent much diminished. But for our present limited purpose, the important point is that for the same reasons it is going to be equally difficult to maintain that the world is *not* a good place overall; there simply is no neutral yet comprehensive point of view available to us from which to assess that it is a bad place, all things considered, as distinct from a place in which there are many bad situations from one or another point of view.

None of these considerations deals with morally bad behaviour. From the moral point of view this can have no redeeming features; and we would surely wish that any assessment of our world would at least give the moral point of view very considerable weight. Now it has often been argued that the immoral behaviour of others can call forth patience, even heroism, and can inspire other admirable dispositions, such as being forgiving, or generous. Of course this is true. But it is also true that all too often human neglect leads to people dying alone and in misery, many of them wholly unnoticed, with absolutely no payoff in terms of heroism or generosity. In any case it does not seem to me that one could defend the overall goodness of the moral world on such grounds. In most views of ethics, one cannot justify doing something which is clearly in itself wrong because it might have good effects. If we are to judge that the world is overall good, it will have to be despite the horrendous behaviour of tyrants and exploiters, betrayers and thieves, and not because the actions of such people can be justified.

Another possible approach to asking whether we believe our world is good or bad, all things considered, is to try some thought experiments using comparisons. One might ask, is Earth, all things considered, a better place than our moon, or Mars? On those bodies there are, to our knowledge at least, no moral evils, no predatory animals, no illness, infection or violence. Of course, neither is there life or art or love. Is the loss of these too high a price to pay for the avoidance of so many evils? Or, to bring the comparison closer to home, rather than considering barren and lifeless places like our moon or Mars, one might think of Earth before animals had evolved, and try to paint an idyllic picture of a verdant paradise in which there is no pain or malice of any kind. Or we could even try to compare Earth with animals before humans evolved with the earth as we now know it: in those distant times there was no moral evil — which is the kind of evil about which we are clearest; so would Earth then have been better or worse, all things considered, than it is today?

I find it difficult to take such questions really seriously, so obvious does it seem to me that the value of the huge range of human cultures and their achievements is so rich as to be worth having at almost any price. But while it is so easy for me to say that in the comfort of my study, would the comparative values seem nearly so clear to the starving disease-ridden and hopeless poor of our own planet in our own times? Once again, questions about the point of view from which such matters are to be assessed become pressing.

To sum up. I have argued that we have no clear access to any cosmic point of view from which all these competing needs can be assessed and judgement made as to whether or not our planet as a whole is a good thing or a bad thing, all things considered. The theist will rightly urge that it is precisely God's point of view which is the ultimate standard of reference for all judgements of good and evil. An old German hymn expresses one part of this view, in connection with the time of one's death.

> Gottes Zeit ist die allerbeste Zeit:
> in ihm leben, weben, und sind wir,
> solange er will;
> in ihm sterben wir zur rechten Zeit,
> wenn er will.

> *God's time is the best time of all:*
> *In Him we live and move and have our being,*
> *for as long as he wills it.*
> *In Him we die, when the right moment comes,*
> *when he wills it so.*

If there is a God perhaps in some overall sense this is true. But even if there is a God, it by no means follows that we have access to God's point of view in anything like the detail we would need if we were to be able to work out the best time for each of us to die. Even when we are judging the pros and cons of our ordinary decisions, asking whether the benefits of taking a course of action outweigh the disadvantages of trying to apply whatever criterion we use to help to resolve cases of moral conflict, we often find those judgements extremely hard to make. Philosophers and welfare economists who have tried to formulate more precise methods of calculating in such cases would be the first to admit that there simply is no method of doing so which does not in the end rest on preferences which themselves might be called in question. When these problems are encountered in a cosmic context and we are asked to judge whether our world is a good or bad place overall I do not myself see that any judgement can be given with much confidence. For all we can show to the contrary, this might well be a good world overall.

CHAPTER FOUR

A BETTER WORLD?

I have argued that there is no evidence which forces us to conclude that the world is bad overall. I have talked about 'the world' meaning 'the Earth' and said nothing about the universe as a whole, since there seems to me to be no reason to suppose that our estimate of the universe overall will be systematically different from our estimate of this world. I have also argued that if it is true that even one of the required conditions for blameworthiness cannot be shown to be true where God is concerned, then The Problem has been to that extent defused; for if God cannot be blamed, then there are no grounds to argue that no informed and intellectually honest person can believe in a good God who created a world like ours.

However, even if all that is along the right lines there is plenty more to be said. Someone who has suffered in a way that seems quite needless might still feel that this certainly cannot be the best that God can do. God is, after all, supposed to be omnipotent. There are in fact two issues involved in such a complaint, and not just one. The first of these might well threaten to undermine the conclusion reached in the last chapter. The argument was that if what God has done is good, all things considered, then God cannot be blamed; and in defence of this criterion it can be argued that that is exactly the attitude most of us take to the assessment of human conduct. True, the classical utilitarians seem to have required that our duty should be to do whatever would *maximise* the resulting benefits. But this position has often seemed unduly rigorist, ignoring as it does our commonsense view that there is a distinction between acting as duty requires and acting 'over and above the call of duty', as the phrase goes. We are not doing wrong in simply doing our duty; moral heroics are not required of us, immense though our admiration is for people who do act in such ways. But might it not be argued that even if we do routinely distinguish between an action to which there is no moral objection and one which is unusually admirable, this distinction should certainly not be applied to God? God should act not merely in complete accordance with our normal moral standards, but in accordance with our highest moral ideals. After all, God is believed to be good without limit. I believe that this argument has to be taken seriously. Even if in general we have little alternative to thinking of God in human terms, we also try not to apply our human terms to God in such a way as to bring God down to our level more than is absolutely unavoidable. I think our instinctive complaint that God should not be content with less than the very best he can do is entirely reasonable.

But if that is the case, then The Problem is not defused simply by pointing out that we have no good reason to deny that all things considered the world is a good one. We need to show that there is no good reason to deny that it is the *best possible* world, as Leibniz famously claimed. This does indeed seem a daunting requirement, for we don't have to try very hard to think of quite a few useful suggestions we could make to improve things. Surely a better world is possible?

Leibniz denied that a better world is possible. He argued that the infinite goodness of God makes it inevitable that God will always do the best possible action; so not merely will this be the best world that could possibly be created, but to create this world must be better than not to create at all. However, this particular argument that ours must be the best possible world will work only if there is no reason to doubt the existence of God; and the case for denying that there is a God will seem to many people to be extremely strong. For this reason we have to start from the bottom up and discuss whether we can see that a better world would indeed have been possible, rather than taking the Olympian point of view which Leibniz felt able to adopt to show that it would not. David Hume does just that.

Hume's *Dialogues on Natural Religion* is one of the most entertaining texts in philosophy of religion, and contains a set of objections to the suggestion that this might be the best possible world. He succeeds very well in capturing what many people would instinctively want to say. In general, Hume places no restrictions whatever upon what a Perfect Being might be expected to do. His natural starting point is simply to say that, since God is omnipotent – by which he means that God can do anything at all – then absolutely *any* world is a possible world for God. I shall return to the details of his suggestions presently.

First, there are good reasons to think that understanding divine omnipotence is not nearly as simple a matter as Hume's approach would make out. Uncontroversially, there are some things which God cannot do because God is not part of the physical world. God cannot, therefore, walk with Adam in the garden, or lead Israel out of Egypt with a mighty hand and an outstretched arm, nor can he wear a beard and sit upon a throne – God can do none of these things other than in a metaphorical sense.[1] We must not be misled by our use of metaphors into a mistaken view of what is possible for God. When Thomas Aquinas discusses God's omnipotence he is interested in trying to sort out what powers God can be literally said to have.[2] He starts off by remarking that 'what is possible for someone' depends on their nature; so to say that God is omnipotent means that God can do everything a god can do. He promptly goes on to say that, while that is indeed true, it is also extremely unhelpful. Instead, he suggests as an improvement that God can do whatever is 'absolutely possible'. This term still needs clarification,

---

1   Of course Christians believe that God-in-Jesus can walk the earth, speak, hear and sleep. But Jesus did these things because he was a human being like us. Appendix I offers a few further remarks on the role of metaphorical language in describing God.
2   His discussion is to be found in the *Summa Theologiae* I, q. 25.

but Aquinas certainly is not writing a blank cheque here. He does not believe that everything we could think of or imagine must be absolutely possible, even for God. He gives two examples: one is the absolute impossibility of God creating a man-donkey; and the other is the absolute impossibility of God undoing the past. But how does Aquinas know that these are impossible, even for God?

It would at least at first sight appear that he takes the basic test to be whether or not the description of something involves a contradiction. The meaning of 'goat' – 'a small woolly animal with little horns' etc. contradicts the definition of 'stag', 'a large fleet-footed animal with great antlers'; again if the past is changed, then (at least so goes the argument) we would be faced with saying both that 'The Battle of Hastings took place in 1066' and saying that 'There never was a Battle of Hastings'. Nothing can be possible, even for God, if it involves contradictions like these. Is this a good test? I think that understood in this way it just isn't. The reason is that it is at least largely up to us what we will count as a contradiction and what we will not count as a contradiction. Of course, as everyone starts off by saying, you can't have a square circle because it's a contradiction in terms. But consider; 'parallel' can be defined in such a way that it is contradictory to suppose that parallel lines can meet; but for some purposes, it is more helpful to define it in such a way that parallel lines meet at infinity. Depending on what we wish to use mathematics for, we can define its terms as we please.

The same, strictly speaking, is true for ordinary terms. The word 'atom', from the Greek root meaning 'cannot be divided', is no longer defined in that way, because we wish to use the term to refer to the smallest unit of a particular kind of substance, but not thereby to say that that unit cannot be subdivided into smaller particles; the atom of hydrogen can be divided into sub-atomic particles not one of which is hydrogen – in that sense hydrogen does not come in smaller parcels than atoms of hydrogen; but the hydrogen atom can be divided. Analogously, we do not wish to define whales as fish, and we no longer wish to include 'white' in the definition of 'swan' as a

European in the middle ages might have been happy to do. We redefine words in such a way that when we use them they will reflect what we take to be really possible in our world – and when we discover that some things are after all possible which we used to think impossible, we redefine our terms to avoid the appearance of contradiction when we use those words. 'Black swan' is fine. To rely on contradiction as the test is to do things almost the wrong way round. Our words enshrine the knowledge and interests we currently have; and since we are interested in being able to interact in a satisfactory and predictable way with our world, we give our words meanings which reflect what we have learned about that world. Our grasp of what seems possible and impossible is what determines which expressions we do and do not take to be contradictory, not the other way round. Aquinas was rather more confident that his vocabulary fitted the world exactly than we would be in an age of rapid scientific discovery. He could assume that the logical relations between words captured pretty well what was and was not feasible in practice. We cannot be so confident.

What would we say if some Edinburgh researchers managed to cross a goat and a stag? Aquinas would have assumed that to be quite impossible, and that the contradictory expression 'goat-stag' was a reflection of that impossibility, and offered an easy test for what was and was not possible in fact. But if we were convinced by the research, we would then decide to use the terms 'goat' and 'stag' in such a way that 'goat-stag' no longer counted as contradictory. A woman in North Wales believes that her cat mated with a dog: the local paper carried a photograph of her cat accompanied by what are indeed slightly odd looking offspring: 'Cogs', 'Dats'? Experts who are sceptical about whether this could possibly have happened do not rely on the notion of contradiction, for the very good reason that we do not actually know what to call them; they are reported to be conducting DNA tests; and depending on the outcome of those tests we might or might not then wish to revise our vocabulary.

A Better World?

At least as I write this, Aquinas's example, to have a man-donkey, is still thought to be an absolute impossibility, and the two words are used in such a way that 'a man-donkey' is a contradiction in terms. But some geneticists are proposing some kind of merger between human and animal cells; so whether 'man-donkey' is a contradictory expression might be just as bad a test for what is absolutely possible as 'black swan' would have been for Aquinas. We simply do not know.

But of course we can fantasise. My own Scottish version of Aquinas's man-donkey involves an image of herds of naturally tartan sheep — Hunting Stuarts, Black Watches, MacDonalds, each safely grazing in their separate fields somewhere in the Scottish Borders. A tourist attraction, and a real boost for the kilt industry. Sci-fi dramas can contain requests such as 'Beam me up Scotty!' which plainly, in that context, are not intended to be requests for the impossible. Recent films have involved people travelling forwards and backwards through time and have played with the idea of what would happen if someone went backwards in time and killed his grandparents. And as the Greeks had chimaeras, and Aquinas had God undoing the past (in both cases claiming that they were talking about things that were 'absolutely impossible' and hence could not be done even by God), so other philosophers too have indulged their imaginations. William of Ockham suggested that anything we could clearly distinguish conceptually could be actually produced by God. Smoke without a fire was no trouble at all; but God could make us actually see a non-existent battle (since the experience of a battle is conceptually distinct from the battle itself); and Descartes wondered about mountains existing without any valleys. Descartes explicitly warned his readers:

> In general we can assert that God can do anything that is within our grasp, but not that he cannot do what is beyond our grasp. I would be rash to think that our imagination reaches as far as his power.[3]

3   Letter to Mersenne, 11 April 1630.

Descartes thus cautions us against limiting God's power to what we can believe or imagine, which indeed is reasonable enough; but even for Descartes this did not amount to saying that anything we can imagine, God can do. No such sheep, Scotty!

But if the meanings we give to our words and the contradictions which arise as a consequence of those meanings, or if our current beliefs or our best imaginings are not reliable guides to what can be done 'absolutely', as distinct from done by us or done with our current technology, then what do we know about the powers of an omnipotent God? I think the fundamental answer is that we know comparatively little. Descartes is right: what we see around us must all be absolutely possible, since it is actually here. I suppose, too, that we know that other versions of this world are possible in so far as they depend upon free choices people have made or will make. A world in which I am not writing this sentence at this moment in time was once an absolutely possible world. I suppose, similarly, that there are reasonable grounds for predicting what will happen to our world climate depending on the various choices we humans might possibly make. It might still be possible to put a stop to the most damaging versions of global warming. Again, taking the basic laws of our universe as a starting point we can extrapolate and produce versions of what the universe might have been like had one or other of the constants in our universe been somewhat different.

Descartes' generosity towards God's power notwithstanding, it has to be said that the more the projections we make differ from the world as we know it, the less sure we can be that we are still talking about what is absolutely possible. I have already mentioned a good example of this, concerning the nature of time. The ancient debate about undoing the past, or the modern one about whether time travel generally is possible, is still perhaps not conclusively settled. The all-but-unanimous view has hitherto been that this was absolutely impossible – even for God. However, Stephen Hawking has recently questioned whether we can be so sure. But there are problems, as he says: 'One of these is, if sometime in the future, we learn to travel in time, why hasn't someone come back from the future, to tell us how to do it?'

The examples are perhaps less important than the issue of principle involved. We have only a very incomplete grasp of what might be absolutely possible; but at least all our efforts to clarify matters in that direction suggest that in the universe as we know it there are many things which are absolutely impossible.

But why should that be a limitation on the powers of God? As Descartes neatly pointed out, the answer to this question is complex. The first and clearer part of the answer is that if we ask whether God could do something which is quite unlike what we know him to have done – say, produce a completely different kind of creation – then surely Descartes is right: we cannot assume that the limits of the power of God happen to coincide with what we now experience or are able to imagine. However, a universe like ours, so far as we can tell on the basis of the scientific knowledge we have, comes as a package. The various aspects of our world are very tightly interlocked, simply because the things in our world interact with one another in ways determined by their various natures. Not, of course, that the laws of nature force things to behave in a fixed way: the laws of nature are not in any sense causal agents; rather they describe the fixed ways in which things of themselves of necessity interact. The more we learn, the more we appreciate how tight the limits of our universe are. If the fundamental forces in our universe were even very slightly different, the substances and materials to which we are accustomed simply would not exist at all. So far as we can tell, it is absolutely not possible to make small-scale changes in the laws of physics which will leave most things much the same, with only selected differences. A radically different creation might well be possible, for all we know; but a very slightly different one seems to be highly unlikely. Whenever we decide to do one thing we thereby exclude other things we might well have done instead. It is the same even with an omnipotent God. Is God's power then limited by the laws of physics? The question is misplaced. Just as the laws of physics are not entities somehow 'out there' limiting the things of our world, still less do they limit God. It is simply that in creating anything physical as we understand that term, God inevitably creates limited, finite things which have the natures they do, rather than different things altogether. A world containing such limited things is a world in which not everything is still possible. To create is inevitably to decide. The laws of physics do not limit God's power: they are simply a way of describing the limitations of the universe which God has chosen to create.

So, back to Hume's suggestions that an omnipotent God could easily have arranged things in our world much better than he has done. We test whether dats or cogs are really possible neither by looking up a dictionary nor by exercising our imaginations, but by doing DNA tests; just so, we do not test Hume's imaginative pictures of a better world just by wishful thinking. Here are some of the suggestions he makes:

> The *first* circumstance which introduces evil is that contrivance or economy of the animal creation by which pains, as well as pleasures, are employed to excite all creatures to action, and make them vigilant in the great work of self-preservation. Now pleasure alone, in its various degrees, seems to human understanding to be sufficient for this purpose. All animals might be constantly in a state of enjoyment, but when urged by any of the necessities of nature such as thirst, hunger, weariness, instead of pain they might feel a diminution of pleasure ...[4]

This suggestion that animals might be driven not by pain but by lesser pleasure is typical of the appeal which an imaginative alternative can have. When one tries to consider it in detail, however,

---

4   *Dialogues on Natural Religion*, XI.

it is much less easy to pin down. One can think of a state such as boredom which might encourage some animal to attempt to alter its situation. But even boredom, although not exactly a pain, would seem at least in some degree undesirable; Hume's suggested 'diminished pleasure' has to be at least a bit more enjoyable than that or it would have to be construed as just a slight pain. Perhaps, then, he has in mind whatever it is that might make one, for instance, say 'No thank you' when offered a further helping of something one has enjoyed, or whatever it is that makes one in the end turn away from a view one is enjoying. Perhaps it is the perception that a pleasure is just on the verge of cloying. The difficulty with this suggestion, though, is that it seems insufficient. Pain warns us about kinds of damage which might require an urgent and decisive response, and it seems unlikely that mere gradual loss of enjoyment would have anything like the immediate motivating power which is often needed. Indeed, in an evolutionary setting one might ask why such animals did not evolve at the expense of animals which are subject to pain; and the most obvious answer is that the pain response is in the end the most advantageous stimulus we could have towards being 'vigilant in the great work of self-preservation'. And if Hume were to reply that there might be another method of producing animals than the evolutionary system to which we are accustomed, the suggestion might be countered by saying that at this point his apparently simple idea has become totally obscure, and its possibility correspondingly uncertain. I think much the same should be said in reply to his third suggestion, that all sentient beings should be so equipped as to be able to avoid all pain – and, presumably, to avoid all the damage which such pain might warn against. At this point, Hume's grasp on what can possibly come about in our world seems to have been entirely lost.

However, there is a very good reason why he might have been untroubled by my insistence on keeping some contact with the possible when speculating as he does. The reason is given in his second suggestion:

> But a capacity of pain would not alone produce pain
> were it not for the *second* circumstance, viz., the
> conducting of the world by general laws; and this
> seems nowise necessary to a very perfect Being … In
> short, might not the Deity exterminate all ill, wherever
> it were to be found, and produce all good, without any
> preparation or long process of causes and effects?

It would be altogether simpler, he suggests, not to have things which
operate according to general laws at all. Hume does not believe we
have evidence which proves that there is any causal necessity in the
world; it just so happens that the world behaves in a regular fashion.
He believes that even as things are there is no built-in necessity why
it should do so, nor why it should continue to do so. It is therefore
not so hard for him to suppose that someone could cut their hand
without any pain at all, or indeed that God could simply arrange
things for the best from everyone's point of view without any
suffering at all. But the cost of taking this proposal seriously would
be that the natures of things – upon which their regular behaviour
and predictability depends – would in fact have nothing to do with
what could actually happen. We would be totally in the hands of a
God whose actions would be the only source of what regularity – if
any – there might be in the universe. Something like this criticism
must underlie Lewis Carroll's description of Alice trying to play
croquet with a flamingo for a mallet, a hedgehog for a ball and
soldiers bending over to form the hoops:

> The chief difficulty Alice found at first was in
> managing her flamingo: she succeeded in getting its
> body tucked away, comfortably enough, under her arm,
> with its legs hanging down, but generally, just as she
> had got its neck nicely straightened out, and was going
> to give the hedgehog a blow with its head, it *would* twist

itself round and look up in her face, with such a puzzled expression that she could not help bursting out laughing: and when she had got its head down, and was going to begin again, it was very provoking to find that the hedgehog had unrolled itself, and was in the act of crawling away; besides all this, there was generally a ridge or furrow in the way wherever she wanted to send the hedgehog to, and, as the doubled-up soldiers were always getting up and walking off to other parts of the ground, Alice soon came to the conclusion that it was a very difficult game indeed.[5]

The regular predictable world goes haywire. Suppose we are trying to implement some longer-term plan – anything from investigating the nature of the atom to more everyday things like getting married. On the Humean suggestion, what would happen might or might not have much connection with what we were trying to do; it would depend entirely upon whether implementing our plan would ever cause pain to someone, or, less ambitiously, would at least produce a good world overall. But the first seems totally impracticable, and the second might not, for all we know, be at all different from the world we have. Either way, it is difficult to see how we could be responsible for anything at all that happened.

Hume's two final points are both concerned with rather smaller-scale changes which he politely suggests that God, as loving father, would have been well-advised to make.

It seems scarcely possible but that some ill must arise in the various shocks of matter and the various concurrences and opposition of general laws; but this ill would be very rare were it not for the *third* circumstance ... the great frugality with which all the

---

5   *Alice's Adventures in Wonderland.*

powers and faculties are distributed to every particular being ... An *indulgent* parent would have bestowed a large stock to guard against accidents ...

The *fourth* circumstance whence arises the misery and ill of the universe is the inaccurate workmanship of all the springs and principles of the great machine of nature ... None of these parts and principles, however useful, are so accurately adjusted as to keep them precisely within those bounds in which their utility consists; but they are, all of them, apt, on every occasion, to run into one extreme or another.

Hume calls for just those small adjustments which seem to be excluded by everything that we have recently learned about the laws of nature. From what we have learned, it appears that even the smallest alteration of 'the springs and principles of the great machine of nature' would produce quite incalculably large effects, some of which would make a world like ours quite impossible. Hume amusingly tries to convince us that, as he puts it, 'This world ... is faulty and imperfect, compared to a superior standard, and was only the first rude essay of some infant deity who afterwards abandoned it, ashamed of his performance'. But any specification of the laws needed to achieve such a standard is left entirely vague, and we have no grounds for supposing that it is absolutely possible even to devise such a standard.

My tentative conclusion would therefore be this. It might indeed be that, for all we know, God could create – and indeed might in fact have created – a universe very different from this one, or conceivably a very different planet from this one. As Descartes says, we should not assume God's power is limited by our imaginations. But if such a world or universe were very different indeed, it seems to me that we would in all likelihood not be able to make any meaningful comparison between it and our own. Comparisons require that the things to be compared can be seen as lying on a common scale. That is why we can readily imagine worlds only slightly different from this one which might be better, maybe even much better. But the difficulty here is that at least there is a good case for saying that it would not be possible simply to fine-tune or to tweak – to update Hume's metaphor somewhat – this universe, since such small changes in the laws or the starting conditions would, as far as we can tell, have very radically different effects and not just the selective improvements we might have had in mind. There are no coherent grounds for insisting that omnipotence can achieve results which we know to be physically impossible given what God has in fact decided to do.

So we are left with the possibility that this might indeed be as good a world as can be had. The good news is that, if this conclusion is a reasonable one, then it is reasonable to believe that The Problem need not be fatal to traditional theism. The bad news is that in an important sense The Problem is still with us; none of the miseries which provoked the complaints are likely to be assuaged by assurance that maybe this was the best that could be done.

CHAPTER FIVE

HOW MUCH DID GOD KNOW?

The focus of the previous chapter was on what is often termed 'natural evil' – all the misfortunes which occur because of the mere workings of the non-human universe. The non-human universe, it is assumed, works in a determinist way. Even in the realm of sub-atomic physics where it is a widely held view that there are undetermined events, there is at any rate a statistical regularity. As a result, if we assume that God knew the ways in which the natures of the various items in creation would of necessity interact with one another, and that God knew the starting conditions exactly, then God would thereby know all the subsequent stages through which the non-human universe would develop over time. In the fullest possible sense, then, God is responsible for what he knowingly did in creating the non-human world.

Within the world of human activities, however, things might be different. First, there are those who believe that even human choices are determined by the very features of our bodies and our upbringing which have made us who we are. There are things which simply happen to us, of course; but on this view the difference between what just happens to and in us, and things which we voluntarily do is that our voluntary behaviour is not subject to any *external* coercion; it is determined in accordance with our beliefs and our desires at the time. On this account, for behaviour to be free it is not necessary that at the time we could have acted differently. On this hypothesis, God knows all our voluntary actions as well as, and in just the same way as, God knows every other event in the universe. In creating things as he has done, and in knowing the starting conditions of the universe, he thereby also knows how everything subsequently plays out. On this account, God is as fully responsible for the moral ills of the world as he is for the natural ones, since both are tied into the way a universe of this kind inevitably behaves; and this is known to God with complete precision. Someone who wishes to exonerate God from responsibility for the moral evils of the world will have to rely on what has already been said about the reasonable possibility that, despite all the human malice in the world, the world is good overall and could not be better. This might indeed be the case, since it might simply not be possible to evolve a race of humans who, statistically, are any more morally upright than the one we at present have.

Some believers, mistakenly in my view, have taken all this to be an insufficient line of defence. They may be unconvinced by the reasons I have already given for saying that God might be blameless since this may well be a good world overall; and unconvinced even by the claim that for all we know to the contrary it may well be the best possible world of its kind. In any case it might be thought that while it is tolerable to say that God is wholly responsible for the ills of the natural world, it is much less acceptable for a theist to say that God is equally responsible for the moral failures, many of them horrendous, which have occurred in our world. Whatever be the case with the death of a gazelle, or even an illness to a human, there is no getting away from the fact that immoral behaviour is in itself just bad. Hence people have often found it tempting to argue that God is not responsible for moral evils, since a) behaviour which is to count morally must be free in the sense of undetermined; and b) God cannot know in advance of our free choices in the way that God can know about next year's weather. Complex as may be the factors governing weather, they are part of a determined pattern; and an omniscient God would have no problem in knowing that. This whole line of argument is for obvious reasons often called the Free Will Defence. I shall argue that there is a good deal of truth in this view, which certainly explains its attractions; but I believe that the Free

Will Defence is nonetheless flawed and that God cannot be exonerated in that way.

For the Free Will Defence (FWD) to succeed two things have to be true: that God did not cause the immoral actions of any individual; and that God simply in creating such a person had no way of knowing what those actions would be. Let us look at each of these separately.

The first problem for the FWD is that if (as most theists would maintain) God is the cause of everything in the universe, then it appears to follow that God must also be the cause of our free actions. If this were straightforwardly true, then, of course, the FWD would at once collapse; God is either wholly responsible for our behaviour, or is at least responsible in the sense in which someone who gets someone else to do something is responsible for what that person does. The only way of avoiding divine responsibility, and hence blameworthiness, along these lines would be to try to maintain that in either case the person could equally well do something else even given God's causal input sustaining the person in being while they made that choice. This is exactly what Aquinas tries to do. He points out that God's causal input into our world is not at all parallel to the way in which things in the world interact with one another. He is even willing to say that God causes us to choose freely.[1]

Well, perhaps that might be accepted since it is reasonable to suggest that God's causal action is indeed almost totally different from our own; he is not just another part of the universe, interacting with it according to the laws of physics; so it may be that he could get us to do good freely on every occasion. The first difficulty, which, as it seems to me, makes Aquinas' position here untenable, is that in addition Aquinas also wants to make sure that at no point do creatures have any causal effect on God. In particular, therefore, God's knowledge of what we freely do cannot come about by God

1 De Malo 6, ST I, 83, I

as it were creating us and then having to wait to see us do it. Of course, if God is eternal in the sense of timeless, talk of God 'first' doing something and 'then having to wait' etc. will be metaphorical, rather that literal. But the metaphor is still helpful, because it enables us to see more clearly the nature of the causal links involved. Aquinas wants to deny that there are *two* such links in this case – one from God, creating us, and a second stemming from our actions and bringing about God's knowledge of what we do. There is just one causal link: God knows what we freely do by being aware of his own causal input into our actions. I suppose an analogy might be something like that of a javelin thrower who might instantly know whether a throw was a good or a bad one without having to wait to see the javelin come down, just because of how the throw felt. But, of course, that works only because the javelin does not have a mind of its own, and certainly does not decide where it would like to come down. Yet Aquinas wishes to say both that God's causal input leaves us free, but is also sufficient to make God aware of what we freely choose. But if the javelin were really free, then how the throw felt to the thrower would not be enough to tell the thrower where the javelin would come down. The only way of reconciling human freedom with God's omniscience is to accept that God knows what we freely do only by seeing us do it, so to speak. Of course, if God is eternal, he does not have to wait to see what we are going to do. Nevertheless, he cannot know of our free actions just by creating us, independently of what we happen to decide. Our behaviour produces God's knowledge, not the other way round. In itself, I think this is quite an acceptable view.

Well, if one is willing to pay that price, making some of God's knowledge dependent upon creatures like ourselves, does it not seem that the FWD will succeed? If God cannot know 'in advance', so to speak, what we will do if he creates us, he cannot, it would seem, be held responsible for what we in fact do. But things are still not plain sailing for the FWD. We need to ask whether it is in fact true to say that if *each* free choice could be a good one, it follows that *every* free choice could be a good one? If it could, then there obviously is an absolutely possible world which is better than this world, for it would be a world in which there are no moral evils at all. Moreover, it does not seem that it would be subject to the objections raised above against the idea of fine-tuning the natural world. That was not possible because of the fixed natures of things once they have been created as they are. But in the case of genuinely free choices there seems no reason why they could not all be good choices; there would be no need for selective interference with the laws of nature at all. If God did not take this chance, the argument would go, God must surely be to blame.

On the other hand, we do have what is, admittedly, the rather unscientific impression that the incidence of wrongdoing is more or less randomly distributed among human beings; by which I mean that there are extremely few people who rarely or never do anything morally wrong, and extremely few who are so morally corrupt that they hardly ever do anything good. Most of us, it seems, are somewhere in the middle, neither saints nor totally morally corrupt. One might be tempted to conclude that this pattern points to some kind of statistical necessity, and that there must be *some* kind of natural inevitability about it. The chances of a penny coming down heads on any given occasion are even, and for that very reason long strings of successive heads or successive tails become more unlikely the longer they are. In the same kind of way, it might be a natural fact about us that even if on each occasion we could choose to do what is right, we nevertheless all behave morally badly in some degree and with some frequency; and no doubt both of these can be influenced by temperament and upbringing. In that case it may be a natural fact that we are all to some extent moral failures. If so, even though individual choices might be unpredictable it might nevertheless be statistically impossible to have a world in which nobody ever freely did wrong. So God would still be responsible to some extent, since whatever fact about human nature underlies that pattern of behaviour would surely have been known to God in advance of creating our world. The FWD would therefore fail to exonerate God, even if it did establish that there might be no *individual* free decision which God could have known about 'in advance'. God would still have known the overall pattern, ranging from the saintly to the perpetrator of genocide, with most of us in between.

So the Free Will Defence fails. God must have known the general features of our moral world. The theist is therefore thrown back on the earlier arguments. Whether God can be exonerated, or whether he can properly be blamed for creating a world such as ours, must in the end rest on whether the world, with all its moral horrors as well is its moral heroines and saints, can overall be shown to be bad, or at any rate much less good than it might have been. If, as I have argued, neither of those accusations can be made to stick beyond any reasonable doubt, then neither can God be shown to be blameworthy.

Is there then sufficient justification for blaming God for creating a world like ours? If there is, all five of the conditions given on page 32 must be satisfied:

i) The world is a bad world all things considered
ii) God created the world
iii) God knew how the world would work out
iv) God could have created a better world than this
v) God knew he could have created a better world than this.

I have argued that we are not capable of making the overall assessment required to establish the truth of i); indeed, there seem to be good grounds for saying that this might be as good a world as it is possible to create, since a *radically* different world would not be comparable; and a similar but selectively different version of this world might not even be possible. Hence, there is no way of establishing iv); and if one cannot establish iv), it follows that we cannot establish v) either. I have accepted that ii) is true in the required sense, that God is responsible for everything that happens in the world, and that in some sense iii) may also be true, since the Free Will Defence fails to show that God could not have 'foreseen' the moral depravity of humans, even if he could not foresee the free actions of each individual.

In short, the claim that one cannot reasonably believe in a good God who created this world simply has not been established. I have not shown, nor indeed have I tried to show, that the non-believer's position is unreasonable, nor that the believer's view can be shown to be true beyond all reasonable doubt. I think that in such matters our human minds are at the very limits of their powers and total clarity is simply beyond us. I also take the belief that the universe has been created by a good God to be true on the balance of probability. That is what I take religious honesty to require.

Part II

CHAPTER SIX

JUSTIFYING GOD: THE JEWISH BIBLE

To adopt the less ambitious strategy in dealing with The Problem is to be content with showing that there is no good reason why one has to deny that the world has been created by a good God. But I have further suggested that a good reason for restricting ourselves to this comparatively modest goal is that more ambitious strategies very often fail. It is now time to make good that claim. The Jewish and Christian traditions contain many attempts to construct theodicies – ways of showing how it is that God is justified in *each of* his actions, 'most sure in *all* his ways'. By considering several of these attempted justifications one by one I shall endeavour to show either that they fail to speak to us because we no longer share the views and practices of the culture in which they were first formulated; or that they are positively harmful in that they reinforce an immoral picture of God; or, in some cases, that they are both alien and harmful. My criticism is not to be taken as a rejection of the motives which encouraged people to justify God's actions in detail. It is after all the very commitment to a single good God which makes some response to The Problem so urgent for any honest believer. Rather my point will be that most theodicies appear to justify God by making God out to be rather less than good; that is why they are positively harmful. Better an admission of ignorance, provided that belief in God can be shown to be rational and honest in the first place, than an attempt to overcome that ignorance in ways which will make belief in God's goodness less than coherent.

Is God to Blame?

i)   The Problem at its simplest

Almost throughout the Jewish Bible, the various writers show a concern to explain why it was that their world and their history was afflicted by so many ills: death, sin, defeat by their enemies, pain and suffering, plague, rejection by God. The various accounts open to polytheist religions – the powers of Good and Evil in perpetual conflict, or the antics of capricious gods taking vengeance on one another's human protégés – which were almost the norm in many of the surrounding cultures in Mesopotamia, Egypt and Greece – were of course not available to the mainstream monotheist tradition of the Jewish people. Indeed the opening two chapters of Genesis are by way of being a monotheist manifesto, written precisely as an uncompromising rejection of polytheism.[1] There is to be no question of the good aspects of the world being created by a good god, and the bad aspects by a bad god. At every stage of the creation narrative in Genesis, the point is not to provide a 'scientific' account – creationist or any other – of how the world came into being; it is to insist on the fact that the one God who made everything saw at every stage that it was good. When all was finished, God rested, completely satisfied with what had been done. The key truth on which those first two chapters insist is that our world is the good world given to us by a single sovereign God, a God who has an especial care for the human race made in God's own image.

Of course, it is precisely this uncompromising starting point which produces the need to account for the misfortunes of a world where everything had seemed to be set fair. The list of such misfortunes is both long and varied. In chapters 3 and 4 of Genesis alone, explanations are sought for such varied ills as our human propensity to sin, the pains of childbearing, a woman's desire for a husband despite the fact that he has now degenerated into being her ruler rather than

---

1   The 'Let us ...' in 1:26 is thought to be a reference to the heavenly court; in 1:27 God alone creates.

her equal, sexual shame, the unremitting toil of obtaining the necessities of life, blood feuds, death and the supposedly unfortunate lack of legs in snakes. In each case, the explanation is the same: creatures, human and angelic, have chosen to disobey God, and are punished for so doing. Yet even in these early chapters of Genesis, God is depicted also as forgiving and caring: Cain is protected against his enemies,[2] and God makes a covenant with Noah which extends well beyond Noah's own lifetime and covers God's relationship to the whole human race.[3] These examples are probably not the most ancient in the Bible, but they are typical of many others. As a generalisation it can be said that this pattern is by far the most prominent: evils are a punishment for sin, yet God nevertheless is ready to offer a way back. But the details vary considerably.

Before we look at the details, however, it is worth reflecting a bit on the general pattern. It is assumed that everything which we humans find difficult or regrettable must be given a divine explanation. Whether all the items in the list given in the previous paragraph are in fact part of The Problem is not discussed, but taken as obvious. Clearly we would not ourselves think of the leglessness of snakes as part of The Problem of Evil; and even human death is not so without qualification. That in our world it is hard work to carve out a fulfilled human life for ourselves is perhaps more open to discussion; could and should God have made a world in which everything was effortlessly blissful as in some mythical Eden? Again at any rate in these passages the punishment involved seems to be tied to a direct act of disobedience; there is little explicit appeal to any abstract idea of justice or morality independent of God's command. God has every right to punish because it is God whose authority has been flouted. Similarly, acts of pardon or generosity on God's part are entirely in his power to give or to refuse.

2   Gen 4:15.
3   Gen 6:18, 8:15–9:17.

Other passages in the Jewish Bible present an altogether more complex picture.

ii) Punishment for injustice as well as infidelity

In the book of Amos, two grounds for punishing Israel are constantly run together: the first is a combination of infidelity and ingratitude to the God who brought them out of Egypt. Thus Amos can write:

> Hear this word that the Lord has spoken against you,
> O people of Israel, against the whole family that I
> brought out of the land of Egypt:
> You only have I known
> of all the families of the earth,
> therefore I will punish you
> for all your iniquities[4]

The suggestion is that the crime is fundamentally one of ingratitude. But in the same book there is a notably different emphasis, where the Lord's complaint is that the people

> Trample upon the needy,
> And bring to ruin the poor of the land[5]

Here God is not punishing people for lacking in respect or obedience to himself; he is upholding basic standards of justice – *human* rights, as we might say. The same emphasis is to be found in Isaiah:

> Justice is turned back,
> and righteousness stands at a distance,

4   Amos 3:1-2.
5   Amos 8:4.

for truth stumbles in the public square,
and uprightness cannot enter.
Truth is lacking,
and whoever turns from evil is despoiled.
The Lord saw it, and it displeased him
that there was no justice.
He saw that there was no one,
and was appalled that there was no one to intervene.
So his own arm brought him victory,
and his righteousness upheld him.
...
According to their deeds so will he repay
wrath to his adversaries, requital to his enemies.[6]

Similarly in Ezechiel:

Because the land is full of bloody crimes and the city full of violence, I will bring the worst of the nations to take possession of their houses; I will put an end to the arrogance of the strong, and their holy places shall be profaned. When anguish comes they will seek peace, but there shall be none. Disaster comes upon disaster, rumour follows rumour; they shall keep seeking a vision from the prophet; instruction shall perish from the priest and counsel from the elders. The king shall mourn, the prince shall be wrapped in despair, and the hands of the people of the land shall tremble. According to their way I will deal with them; according to their own judgements I will judge them; and they shall know that I am the Lord.[7]

6   Is 59:14-18.
7   Ez 7:23-27.

Is God to Blame?

Jeremiah spells it out in deliberately disgusting terms:

> And if you say in your heart, 'Why have these things
> come upon me?'
> It is for the greatness of your iniquity that your skirts
> are lifted up
> and you are violated.
> Can Ethiopians change their skin,
> or the leopards their spots?
> Then can you also do good,
> who are accustomed to do evil.
> I will scatter you like chaff
> driven by the wind from the desert,
> This is your lot, the portion I have measured out for
> you,
> says the Lord,
> Because you have forgotten me and trusted in lies.[8]

From our moral point of view, these passages present several problems. Even allowing for some degree of rhetorical exaggeration, the scale of the punishments seems rather to exceed the crimes: and there is no suggestion that the infliction of these punishments would have any curative effect on the people concerned. The punishment is not an attempt to rehabilitate the offenders; its function is either simply retributive – 'According to their way I shall do to them, and according to their own judgements I will judge them' – or is an expression of divine outrage at such immoral behaviour. There is a general assumption that the crimes are so terrible that the dire threats to humiliate and degrade the perpetrators are entirely justified.

There is a high level of generalisation involved. It is of course necessary to remember that some of these passages are poetry, not to be interpreted too literally or pressed to deal with matters of detail.

8   Jer 13:22-25.

It is also true that the prophets were most often speaking to their society as a whole rather than to any individuals. When a prophet rebukes an individual, such as Solomon or David, the circumstances are made very clear. But the condemnations of the behaviour of the chosen people in general are blanket condemnations; and by the same token, the threats or punishments invoked are also blanket punishments. The assumption would be that if the people as a whole are guilty, then every individual shares in the collective guilt. There is no general assumption that divine punishment, if it is to be just, must affect only the guilty individuals.

However, this is certainly not always the way in which it is presented. When King Solomon was persuaded by his foreign wives to worship their gods, 'the Lord was angry with Solomon because his heart had turned away from the Lord'. The Lord then said this:

> Since this has been your mind and you have not kept my covenant and my statutes that I have commanded you, I will surely tear the kingdom from you and give it to your servant. Yet for the sake of your father David I will not do it in your lifetime; I will tear it out of the hand of your son. I will not, however, tear away the entire kingdom, but I will give one tribe to your son for the sake of my servant David and for the sake of Jerusalem which I have chosen.[9]

The entire passage is an attempt by the writer to square what he knew about historical events – the actual course of the succession, and the splitting of the northern Kingdom of Israel from Judah and Jerusalem – with his general theological views. History must be shown to be brought about *in detail* by God influencing human choices in accordance with criteria founded upon the Torah. The attempt to make theological theory square with the known course of events is highly

---

9   I Kings 11:11-13.

problematic from two points of view. First, it raises problems about human responsibility as contrasted with the divine action. To put this in terms of the Free Will Defence discussed above in Part I, it presents human freedom in a way which undermines any answer to The Problem of Evil which relies on the independence of human actions from God. The older view firmly places upon God all responsibility for the way in which human beings are treated. Second, and most serious, it is clear that the wrong people are punished.

The history of the relationship between King Ahab of Israel and the prophet Elijah follows similar lines.[10] Once again, it is God who determines the outcomes of the battles and who through the prophet criticises the actions of Ahab; once again, the king is led astray by a foreign woman to kill Naboth and take possession of his vineyard. However, though he is described as one who had done evil before the Lord such as nobody else had done, and though Elijah very properly denounces him, the story concludes as follows:

> When Ahab heard these words, he tore his clothes and put sackcloth over his bare flesh; he fasted, lay in the sackcloth, and went about dejectedly. Then the word of the Lord came to Elijah the Tishbite: 'Have you seen how Ahab has humbled himself before me? Because he has humbled himself before me, I will not bring the disaster in his days; but in his son's days I will bring the disaster on his house.'[11]

Repentance, then, is relevant to God's willingness to inflict punishment, which Ahab might regard as no more than is morally appropriate. However, this moral concern does not extend to Ahab's son; or, it does so only because, as will appear, Ahaziah was no better than his father had been, and hence would deserve whatever was coming to him.

10 I Kings 16:29-34, 21:1–22:29.
11 I Kings 21:27-29.

It is surely evident from this that the framework into which the history is cast is fundamentally governed by a concern to find a theological explanation for the details of what happened, an explanation which can somehow be shown to square with the Torah in which God's law was set out. The writer needs to find a theodicy which will show that God is in control and his actions justified. He finds it in the suggestion that God arranges worldly events in accordance with his laws no matter what human beings themselves might try to achieve. At least from our point of view, though not indeed from that of the Jewish historian who employs this theology of history, the God who emerges is in some ways demeaned rather than vindicated, and the attempt to vindicate God leads instead to what, again by our standards, amounts to a disreputably cavalier attitude to the truths of historical explanation.

These ancient examples are in some ways crude, and may seem quite irrelevant to our contemporary ways of dealing with The Problem. But in our own day, to take but one example, there are still people who invoke just such explanations for the advent of AIDS; it is God's punishment for sin, and the fact that the punishment affects hundreds of thousands of innocent people as well as sinners is not considered to be any objection to this view. Such a theodicy is surely intellectually disreputable as well as being morally outrageous. It might perhaps be possible to provide a theodicy which accounts for such human suffering, but the results of insisting that we absolutely have to find something of the kind can produce some quite dreadful results.

iii) Vicarious punishment

A completely different type of issue is raised by texts in the central section of the Book of Isaiah, including what have been called the four Servant Songs.[12] Exactly what do these passages try to do? First, they depict a situation of trial and distress, in which Yahweh is either

12 Is 53:4-6; see also 49:1-6, 50:4-11, and 52:13–53:12.

not properly served or not known at all. Second, they promise that the time will come through the efforts of the Servant when all the nations will be brought out of darkness into the light; they will return to a restored land in which they can once again worship God in justice and in truth. In a general way, therefore, they express distress and agony at their misfortunes, and confidence that the power of God can restore his world to the state in which God intended it to be. The problems and failures of the human condition will be resolved by the power of God. In most of these passages The Problem is not focused on the idea that it is God's behaviour which needs to be justified; the implication is that our unfortunate state has come about because of our failings; and that God's part in any of this does not need any justification. On the contrary, God is the *goel*, the family member coming to help us.[13] This picture of God as bound to us by the closest of ties, and hence bound to come to our assistance, is especially prominent in this part of the book of Isaiah. But apart from implying that God is powerful, the word *goel* in itself carries no other implications about *how* it is that we are freed, liberated or empowered.

So what is said here in Isaiah about *how* this liberation and empowerment of the human race is to be brought about? In the first instance, God helps us simply by exercising his power to change us and our world:

> The Lord is the everlasting God,
> the Creator of the ends of the earth.
> He does not faint or grow weary;
> his understanding is unsearchable.
> He gives power to the faint
> and strengthens the powerless.

---

13 The word is often translated as 'redeemer', and the metaphor is live in Is 52:3, where the people were sold for nothing, and will be redeemed without money. But the word need not have these financial overtones at all: it could equally mean 'avenger' or 'liberator'.

> Even youths will faint and be weary
> and the young shall fall exhausted;
> but those who wait for the Lord shall renew their
> strength,
> they shall mount up with wings like eagles,
> they shall run and not be weary,
> they shall walk and not faint.[14]

God will inspire his servant with his Spirit, to preach to the nations.[15]

It is all the more astonishing, then, to move only a few pages further on, where the Servant, instead of going forth in the power of God and inspired with his spirit, is demeaned, subjected to sufferings, wounded, oppressed and killed; and we discover that all this was done in accordance with God's will.

> Surely he has borne our infirmities
> and carried our diseases;
> yet we esteemed him stricken
> struck down by God, and afflicted.
> But he was wounded for our transgressions,
> crushed for our iniquities;
> upon him was the punishment that made us whole,
> and by his bruises we are healed.[16]

It is not clear from the text or from the context whether the Servant is some particular individual or whether the reference is to the people of Israel as a whole. Is it one person's vocation to restore all the nations to God? Or is it the vocation of the whole people of Israel to reveal God to the Gentiles? Christian theologians have applied this passage to help Christians to understand the passion of Jesus; Jewish

---

14 Is 40:28-31.
15 Cf. Is 42:1.
16 Is 53:4-5.

theologians have seen in it a way of coming to terms with the history of Jewish suffering down the ages; some of their people suffer to free the others. But there is a problem which is common to both these approaches: how can one person's suffering, or the suffering of some individuals from among the Jewish people, possibly compensate for the wrongdoing of others; or, to put it in specifically Jewish terms, how is a sin-offering supposed to work? Does God demand that somebody suffers to make up for the wrongs done by the others, and does not mind who it is? Can personal guilt ever be erased by what happens to someone else even if that person, or those persons, are somehow seen as representative(s) and even as willing representatives? Is it morally acceptable for anyone, let alone God, to be happy with such an arrangement? Or is the suffering as such not the point? Is it perhaps that the key element is twofold: that someone is prepared to apologise for the wrong that was done and that other persons are willing to be associated with that apology?

These issues which arise from specifically Jewish texts will appear again both in the Christian texts in the Bible and in texts in later parts of the Christian tradition. I propose to look at them in that context, too, before discussing what it might be best to say about them. But meanwhile, it will be helpful to rehearse where we have so far got to, and which issues are still completely unresolved.

1. There is at least an apparent problem which is highlighted by the willingness of many biblical texts to insist that history is ultimately God's doing, and therefore good. Of course any believer in a good creator God must believe at least that the world with all its history is good overall. I hope to have shown already that none of the arguments advanced against this view can claim to have been proved beyond reasonable doubt.
2. The difficulty comes when people try to show that each detail, each individual event in the history of the world, must be good in itself, rather than allowing that some things may in themselves be simply bad. Sometimes biblical writers feel the need to justify

what we might think of as quite ordinary natural facts and events; snakes are legless, childbirth is painful, working with the material world is often physically hard, people do die. They also feel they have to show that God is justified in allowing one thoroughly unpleasant monarch to be replaced by another equally unpleasant one. Purely political and social explanations of such events are thought not to be false, exactly, but as in a religious sense radically insufficient. God must have had some very good reason for permitting each such event. So justifications are offered which are often quite unconvincing. There is a great difference between saying that the world is good overall despite the ills which it contains, and saying that the ills which it contains can be seen to contribute to its goodness.

3. Often the wrong people seem to be being punished: and some of the punishments are, by any standards, far too extreme. The morality implied in this account of punishing is quite terrible, but it seemed acceptable because it was thought essential to show that the moral world was God's world, and that God's justice could be seen to be preserved.

Hence the interim conclusion: the attempt to provide a theodicy leads to accounts which are simply in themselves unbelievable, as well as unacceptable. It is only an interim conclusion, however. There are further biblical texts to be considered, taken this time from the Christian tradition. And there are also some biblical texts which seek to undermine the very notion of trying to produce a theodicy at all.

CHAPTER SEVEN

JUSTIFYING GOD:
THE CHRISTIAN BIBLE

The Problem appears in a somewhat simpler form in the Christian biblical writers. They are perhaps more willing to speak of history in the broadest terms, rather than to try to justify the actions of God in detail in the way the writers of the Jewish Bible did in expounding the history of their people. But although the Christian problematic is usually less specific, it is in an important respect rather more urgent. Most of the earliest Christian biblical writers and many of the earliest Christians were themselves Jews. Their need was above all to make sense of the shameful and humiliating death of the man whom they had come to believe was the promised Messiah. Even if initial expectations of the Messiah had to be purged of an all too political ambition, from the Jewish Christian point of view that was still a very long way from anticipating that the promised Messiah would be humiliated, condemned and crucified. A Messiah was expected in some clear sense to be God's final word to his people and to his creation more generally. So what possible good could come from God's allowing his Messiah to be humiliated and killed? Did Jesus really have to die? In the last analysis, why did Jesus die? How could a good God speak through an event like that? That is the particular focus of The Problem of Evil which haunts almost all the Christian biblical writers, threatening their Christianity if not directly their theism.[1] Much of their work can be seen as attempting to make ultimate sense of that dreadful course of events.

---

1   This threat is central to Luke's description of the state of mind of the two disciples on the way to Emmaus, Lk 24:21.

In considering these attempts, it will be helpful to keep in mind two rather different questions: What did Jesus do? and How did Jesus do it? These two questions can each throw light on the way in which the Christian biblical writers deal with The Problem. To ask what it was that Jesus did will throw light on what these writers believe had gone wrong, and on what they take to be the attitude of God to whatever had gone wrong. Both issues are important clues to the moral picture of God's creation which these Christian writers are taking for granted. They are not worried about the plight of the poor snakes, though most of them still think of death as a punishment. On the other hand, they seem to accept the pains of childbirth as natural rather than as punishment; and can even see them as a suitable symbol for the growth of all creation towards God.[2] Paul does not see any need to tackle the issue of women desiring their own subservience. But they are all deeply concerned with human enslavement to sin, along with all the horrors to which that leads. Once more, moral issues arise, for us if not always for them, in connection with the methods God used to put right whatever it was that had gone wrong. Both these points are central to the project of justifying God.

i)   Paul

Paul employs an extremely wide range of imagery in saying what it was that Jesus did. Since the Reformation, it has been common to place the emphasis on Paul's talk of justification. Here is a central passage:

> But now apart from the law, the righteousness of God has been disclosed and is attested by the law and the prophets, the righteousness of God through faith in Jesus Christ for all who believe. For there is no distinction; since all have sinned and fall short of the

2   See, for example, Rom 8:22, Jn 16:21-22.

glory of God, they are now justified by his grace as a gift through the redemption which is in Christ Jesus, whom God put forward as a [sacrifice of] atonement by his blood, effective through faith. He did this to show his righteousness, because in his divine forbearance he had passed over the sins previously committed; it was to prove at the present time that he himself is righteous and that he justifies the one who has faith in Jesus.[3]

In this passage Paul has several concerns. First, he wishes to show to the Romans that God's salvation includes them, while he reassures the Jews that God is not thereby being unfaithful to his covenant with them. There is no question of God switching allegiance, so to speak, from Jews to Gentiles just because Jews were involved in putting Jesus to death. God is equally generous to both. When Paul speaks of God's 'righteousness' he probably has in mind passages such as Ps 143, where righteousness is linked to God's character in general, and in particular God's faithfulness and generous love. So here Paul links it with God's forbearance in not taking our sins into consideration. Second, the effectiveness of God's generosity comes only through a person's acceptance of Jesus. The end result is variously described by Paul: here it is described as a 'redemption' and as an 'atonement'. The first of these terms is simply equivalent to 'liberation'. 'Atonement' is more complex. But perhaps the best interpretation is that God presents Jesus on the Cross as being himself the place in which our sins are wiped away.[4] In other Pauline contexts what Jesus accomplished is

---

3   Rom 3:21-26.
4   The New Revised Standard Version of the New Testament has 'sacrifice of atonement'; 'sacrifice' is perhaps too strong: the Greek word *hilasterion* refers to any means of atonement, as well as to the 'mercy seat' in the Temple where God's forgiveness is to be found; how the blood of Jesus is involved in the atonement is a further issue.

described as a 'washing clean'.[5] But he can also speak of us 'becoming the righteousness of God'.[6] The point of this is to suggest that we come to be as faithful to God as God is to us – there is a reconciliation which establishes a new Covenant relationship between the believers and God. He piles up images, rather than insisting on any one of them, or taking any one of them in a strictly literal sense. But perhaps most central to his view is the concept of a liberation, leading to adoption, leading to a transformation of believers in Christ. Such texts as the following illustrate a point which Paul makes in many different ways:

> Now before faith came we were imprisoned and guarded under the law until faith would be revealed. Therefore the law was our disciplinarian until Christ came, so that we might be justified by faith. But now that faith has come, we are no longer subject to a disciplinarian, for in Christ Jesus you are all now children of God through faith. As many of you as were baptised into Christ have clothed yourselves with Christ.[7]

> There is therefore now no condemnation for those who are in Christ Jesus. For the law of the Spirit of life in Christ Jesus has set you free from the law of sin and death. For God has done what the law, weakened by the flesh, could not do: by sending his own Son in the likeness of sinful flesh, and to deal with sin, he condemned sin in the flesh, so that the just

---

5   In I Cor 6:11 Paul uses several metaphors in this connection: 'You were washed, sanctified, justified in the name of the Lord Jesus Christ'; and in Eph 5:26 the writer (probably a disciple of Paul's rather than Paul himself) speaks of the way in which Christ 'loved the Church and gave himself up for her, that he might sanctify her, having cleansed her by the washing of water with the word'.

6   2 Cor 5:21.

7   Gal 3:23-25; see also 2 Cor 3:17.

requirement of the law might be fulfiled in us, who walk not according to the flesh but according to the Spirit ... For you did not receive a spirit of slavery to fall back into fear, but you have received the spirit of adoption. When we cry 'Abba, Father', it is that very Spirit bearing witness with our spirit that we are children of God ...[8]

I have been crucified with Christ, and it is no longer I who live, but Christ who lives in me; and the life I live in the flesh I live by faith in the Son of God who loved me and gave himself for me.[9]

Now the Lord is the Spirit, and where the Spirit of the Lord is, there is freedom. And all of us, with unveiled faces, seeing the glory of the Lord as though reflected in a mirror, are being transformed into the same image, from one degree of glory to another, for this comes from the Lord, the Spirit.[10]

Paul takes it as obvious that before Christ we were all helplessly in a state of subjection to sin. Quite why he does this is not so clear: perhaps it is simply an empirical observation about the behaviour of human beings – it's just obvious that we are all sinners; perhaps, too, he argues in a very traditional Jewish way, that death is a consequence of sin, and death is inevitable for us all; and so concludes that all of us are inevitably sinners. At any rate, to put the matter in philosophical terms, he certainly thinks that before Christ our world was deeply in need. Rather less clear is what he thinks of our world as it now is. In some sense he believes that it

8   Rom 8:1-4, 15-16; see also 8:29-30.
9   Gal 2:20.
10   2 Cor 3:17-18.

is better than it was, at least to the extent that believers are said now to be living in the Spirit, though the whole creation is still groaning like a woman in labour.[11] But as his criticisms of many of his own churches makes abundantly clear, he thinks that even among those living in the Spirit there is certainly still plenty of room for improvement. Despite what Christ has done for us and in us, the world is certainly not yet in the final state to which Paul looks forward.

What was it that Jesus had to do in order to achieve our (as yet incomplete) liberation from sin, reconciliation with God and transformation through life in the Spirit? The simple version of the answer given by all the first Christians was that Jesus died and rose again. But it is far from clear what Paul made of this, let alone how we might seek to understand it. What good could a death do?

The first thing which the early Christians did was to look for texts in their Jewish tradition to show that the death of Jesus was at least not quite so appallingly unexpected. 'The stone which the builders rejected has become the corner stone' was one such reassuring text, and 'Thou will not abandon my soul to Hades, nor allow thy holy one to see corruption' was another.[12] At least, perhaps, they could recall that the terrible things that had happened were not totally unprecedented in Jewish history: the people did in the end return from the exile; the ruined Temple had been rebuilt. There was no justification for despairing of God, for God abandons neither his people nor his Son. In thinking along these lines, they were, of course, following in a long-standing tradition of Jewish theological understanding, searching for scriptural texts to shed light on their problem. Their answer was summed up in an early Christian creed which Paul repeats:

11 Rom 8:18-22.
12 Acts 4:11, 2:27. The account in the early chapters of Acts is no doubt idealised somewhat, but probably does represent the general style.

that Christ died for our sins in accordance with the
scriptures, that he was buried, and that he was raised on
the third day in accordance with the scriptures.[13]

However, as we saw in the previous chapter, there are both advantages
and disadvantages in this approach: it is reassuring in that it expresses
the faith that God is ultimately in control; but it is problematic, in
that it also raises immediate problems about how a good God could
arrange for salvation to come about in such an awful way.

Paul often links Jesus' death very closely to his resurrection, and
has his own slant on the connection:

Jesus our Lord ... who was handed over to death for
our trespasses, and was raised for our justification.[14]

It is possible that both these texts contain an allusion to the Servant
Song in Is 53 which we have already mentioned. It is interesting to
notice, though, that the only explicit quotation of that text in the
New Testament, in Mt 8:17, is used in connection with Jesus healing
the sick, to illustrate how willing Jesus was to sympathise with our
sufferings – to take them on board as it were – and to cure them. So
even a reference to the Suffering Servant could be used to make Jesus'
sufferings intelligible, without relying on the notion of vicarious
suffering which that text contained. Paul perhaps is not insisting on
the idea of Jesus' death as a sacrifice in the literal sense, but as a
willingness to share in the sufferings of our world. The emphasis is
on God's generosity rather than on any suggestion that God needed
somehow to be vindicated precisely by Jesus' death. The thought of

13 I Cor, 15:4-5. The Lucan narrative (Lk 24:13-35) of the two disciples on the road to
    Emmaus dramatically presents the way in which those who, unlike the apostles, had not
    seen the risen Christ, had come to belief. Luke recommends to his readers a very similar
    process: reflection on the traditional Jewish scriptures, and on the experience of sharing
    in the Eucharist.
14 Rom 4:25.

the Jewish sin-offering may indeed also be present in Paul's mind even if it is not the central point of the comparison; other Pauline texts elsewhere speak of Christ's death as a fragrant offering and sacrifice,[15] once again casting round in the rabbinical tradition, to which Paul himself was proud to belong, in order to find some categories through which he can say that Jesus' death was not just arbitrarily required by God, but had some intelligible function. To us, who do not have the practice of sacrificing animals to God as part of our culture, this approach may not be at all helpful, let alone congenial. I incline to think that Paul, too, is not using 'sacrifice' in its strong liturgical sense, but in the sense in which we can talk of anything we are prepared to forego in a good cause as a 'sacrifice'; in this way Paul can talk about money collected for the churches as a 'fragrant offering and sacrifice'. Certainly, he does find other ways to put things. He can say that Jesus' suffering and death is not a pain demanded by God in reparation, but the consequence of his coming into our suffering world in solidarity with us; for we live in a world in which suffering is widespread, and death universal. Jesus sharing our suffering is the reliable evidence of his aim, that we shall share in his glory. It is not directly a death to satisfy the justice of God which was crucial, but the obedience and generosity of Jesus.

> Therefore just as one man's trespass led to condemnation for all, so one man's act of righteousness leads to justification and life for all. For as by one man's disobedience the many were made sinners, so too by one man's obedience the many will be made righteous.[16]

15 Eph 5:2, and see also Phil 4:18. Jesus' sufferings and those of his disciples are presented in terms of solidarity and shared obedience to God: see 2 Cor 13:3-4; Col 3:1-4.
16 Rom 5:18-19.

Paul can present even death as a matter of rejoicing precisely because it is shared with Christ – 'we carry in our body the death of Jesus so that the life of Jesus may also be made visible in our bodies'; because we share Jesus' sufferings as he did ours Paul can write of his willingness to 'boast of the cross of Christ by which the world is crucified to me and I to the world'.[17]

So in the end Paul is mostly not intent upon appealing to the notion of vicarious suffering which a strict understanding of sacrifice would involve. The sufferings of Jesus are explained by his willingness to share in the human condition, justified as an act of generosity rather than one of redemption or sacrifice in any strict sense of those terms. He is much more focused upon the way in which believers now live with the life of the risen Christ just as Jesus of Nazareth lived with our life. I think that the ultimate justification which Paul would give for the incarnation is that Jesus was thereby able to be a revelation of God, rather than to be a victim on our behalf. That the Messiah was killed says a great deal about how such a revelation is greeted in a sinful world in which God's truth is likely to be inconvenient. Jesus' death can be understood, but not justified either in human or in divine terms. Paul's categories of thought are sufficiently traditional – he himself emphasises his thoroughly Pharisaic upbringing – for the imagery of sacrifice and sin-offerings to be among the ideas he has in mind. However, he does not spend much time trying to offer a theodicy in that sense at all; his emphasis is on the generosity of Jesus, obedience unto death and on the way in which the gift of the Spirit of the risen Jesus is made available freely to us all.

ii) The Gospels

It is a remarkable fact that the Gospels of Mark, Matthew and Luke also seem to have little interest in showing that the death of Jesus was

17 2 Cor 4:10, Gal 6:14. The same ideas apply to Paul's description of another disciple, Epaphroditus, in Phil 2:25-30.

itself a good thing. Instead what they try to achieve is just what Paul also needed: to be reassured that his death need not have been entirely unexpected. They, like Paul, try to find passages in their Jewish biblical tradition which already suggested that the coming of the Kingdom, God's final triumph in the world, would be achieved only with suffering. They would then be able to say that Jesus 'had to' die, since his death was 'according to the scriptures'. The Gospel of Mark depicts Jesus as teaching precisely that uncomfortable lesson to his disciples; for them to recognise him as Messiah was only half of the truth: they needed to know that his suffering was foreseen. Once again, the saying about the stone rejected by the builders becoming the cornerstone is used, this time to punch home the lesson of Jesus' own parable, in which the owner's son is killed by the tenants of the vineyard. The owner did not *set out* to have his son killed as though that was a key part of what was needed in order for him to take vengeance – he thought the tenants would respect his son; the son was killed simply because the tenants were greedy.[18]

The Gospel of Matthew points out that Jewish biblical texts could be found to confirm even some of the details of the passion of Jesus – the purchase of the field with the money given to Judas[19] and the mocking suggestions that Jesus should save himself.[20] John cites the same psalm as background for the casting of lots for Jesus' garments and the piercing of Jesus' side with a lance.[21] The death of God's chosen one was indeed terrible, but, as with hindsight they could now begin to see, not wholly alien to their own traditions.

So we can understand what the early Christians were and, importantly, were not trying to say. There is no suggestion in any of these Jewish precedents that the deaths referred to were punishments inflicted by God. They are all attributed to the failure of sinful

18 Mk 12:10; also in Mt 21:42, and Lk 20:17.
19 Zech 11:11-14.
20 Ps 22:8.
21 Jn 19:22-24, Ps 22:16-18.

human beings to listen to the words of prophets and those whom God has sent. The tenants of the vineyard are not God's instruments of vengeance, they are simply unscrupulous and ambitious human beings. Even when Jesus says that 'The Son of Man came not to be served but to serve, and to give his life as a ransom for many',[22] the point is not that somehow God has to be repaid his pound of flesh or is like some kidnapper making a ransom demand: the expression in Jewish tradition can be used exactly as we might say that being killed is sometimes 'the price that has to be paid' for telling people an uncomfortable truth. We and they can say that without implying that someone is there waiting to collect the ransom money. The price Jesus had to pay in trying to reveal God to us was that he himself would be killed

In Mark's Gospel, the final climax of Jesus' teaching to his disciples comes just before his passion. It consists of a long warning about how the Christian communities will have to face the same misunderstanding and sufferings which were hanging over Jesus himself. Mark's conclusion is given in the central verse of the chapter: what is required of the disciples is to do what Jesus did, 'to endure to the end'.[23] In this spirit Mark and Luke go on to describe the Last Supper. The bread is the body of Jesus, given for them; the cup is the blood of Jesus, poured out as a covenant for them. The supper was a Passover meal, and in Jewish tradition the Paschal lamb is not an offering sacrificed to make up for their sins; it is a sign of God's covenant, his promise to be with his people as he was when once he freed them from Egypt. They are his people, and he is their God. Hence in Paul's quotation of the early Christian tradition, to share in the Eucharist is to proclaim the death of the Lord until he comes — to express the Passover faith that God will be always with us and keep us safe.[24] When Paul says, 'Christ was obedient unto

22 Mk 10:45.
23 Mk 13:13.
24 1 Cor 11:26.

death, even death on a cross', he is saying that what was valuable was the obedience, not as such the cross; and so too it is for us, since to be committed to such obedience is to be crucified to the world, and to have Christ living in us.[25]

The Gospel of John concludes by saying that it was written so that we may believe and have life in Jesus' name; and from the outset the writer makes it clear it is in this act of believing that salvation for us consists.

> But to all who received him, who believed in his name, he gave power to become children of God, who were born not of blood nor of the will of the flesh, nor of the will of man, but of God.[26]

> For God sent his son into the world not to condemn the world, but that the world might be saved through him. He who believes in him is not condemned. He who does not believe is condemned already.[27]

What Jesus came to do was not to be punished for our sins and so be an all too evident example of God's condemnation of the world; John says instead that he came to offer us freedom from the slavery to sin if only we would accept the truth as revealed in Jesus.

> Jesus then said to the Jews who had believed in him, 'If you continue in my word, you are truly my disciples, and you will know the truth and the truth will make you free.' They answered him, 'We are descendants of Abraham, and have never been slaves to anyone. What do you mean by saying, "you will be made free"?' Jesus answered them, 'Very truly, I say to you, everyone who

25 Phil 2:9-18, 2 Cor 4:10, Gal 6:14.
26 Jn 1:12-13.
27 Jn 4:17-18.

commits sin is a slave to sin. The slave does not have a permanent place in the household; the Son has a place there forever. So if the Son makes you free, you will be free indeed.'[28]

It is not too much to say that the central element of salvation in John's Gospel is indeed our willingness to accept and obey God's Word, just as the Son himself is obedient to all the Father asks of him. In this Gospel, the Eucharist is interpreted in terms of the manna in the desert, which itself in Jewish tradition was a symbol of Israel's grateful obedience to the God who had brought them out of Egypt. And, as in Paul, to accept Jesus in this way is to live in Jesus.[29]

So once again the point of Jesus' death was not as such the suffering, still less the suffering as a punishment for our sins. The good shepherd does lay down his life for his sheep – but not because he takes their guilt upon himself or anything of that kind. That would not make sense.[30] The shepherd does not suffer in their place; he does so to free them from danger; it is in this sense that self-sacrifice is the noblest thing a shepherd can do: 'Greater love than this ...' Similarly, the death of Jesus is his glorification, because it is the final act of his commitment to the truth which he came to reveal: 'For their sake I consecrate myself, that they also may be consecrated in truth.'[31]

The only exception to this general picture is in the Gospel of Matthew, where what is clearly a Passover sacrifice is also said to be 'for the forgiveness of sins', which in Jewish tradition the Passover was not.[32] This text, I believe, represents the only place in the Gospels where there is at least an apparent reference to Jesus suffering as a punishment for our sins, which are forgiven precisely because he suffered; and if this is the point of the text, it does indeed raise the

---

28 Jn 8:31-35.
29 Jn 6.
30 The ancient tradition of a scapegoat is absent from the Christian Bible.
31 Jn 17:19.
32 Mt 24:28.

general issue about whether such vicarious suffering 'instead of someone else' is a morally acceptable way for a good God to remove our sins. Could God not simply forgive? In the next chapter we shall see later tradition trying to grapple with this question.

iii)   The Letter to the Hebrews

This 'letter' is in the form of a homily presumably intended for a Jewish Christian audience. In it there are three principal themes: the superiority of the New Covenant and its one High Priest to the Old Covenant with its priesthood; the unique and unrepeatable sacrifice to God offered by Jesus with his blood; and the reminder that the endurance shown by Jesus has been typical of so many men and women of faith and is therefore a model for us.

Once again, the writer is intent upon looking backwards into Jewish tradition for a set of categories through which to make the violent death of Jesus intelligible. This he does through an elaborate comparison and contrast between the Old Covenant, its priesthood and the many rituals and sacrifices which had to be frequently repeated, and the New Covenant, with its once-and-for-all sacrifice offered by the Son – the 'heir of all things through whom God also created the world', as Jesus is described in the first verse of the homily. The comparison is worked out in great detail.

The conclusion would therefore be that here, in a way which is much more elaborate than the single remark of Matthew about Jesus' blood being shed for our sins, it is precisely as a victim under the New Covenant that Jesus is sacrificed for our sins, once and for all. The violence and the vicarious suffering are key elements in what Jesus did for us. His death was a requirement under the New Covenant, 'a better sacrifice' than animal sacrifices under the Old.[33]

It is true that the analogy is perhaps not to be pressed too hard, since the argument goes on:

---

33   Heb 9:21-23.

> Consequently, when Christ came into the world, he
> said,
> 'Sacrifices and offerings thou have not desired,
> but a body you have prepared for me;
> in burnt offerings and sin offerings you have taken no
> pleasure,
> Then I said "See, God, I have come to do thy will O
> God."'[34]

Jesus' death is no longer seen as a sacrifice in the traditional sense, as elsewhere; what is important is the obedience of Jesus, not as such his bloody death. His body is given to him as a means of expressing his obedience in the most extreme test to which a human being can be subjected. Just that obedient and trusting endurance is celebrated in the procession of Jewish heroes and heroines listed in Chapter 11.

iv) To sum up

It might come as something of a surprise to discover what I believe to be the case: that in Paul and in the Gospels there is little or no attempt to justify the suffering of Jesus as something which serves God's purposes in some way. What these early Christian writers wanted was to show that their faith in a Messiah who had died a shameful death could not simply be dismissed as a nonsense in their traditional Jewish terms. So they searched their scriptures for some reassurance that such a terrible event might after all not be totally surprising. The outcome of this search, with which for the most part they were satisfied, was that they could be confident that God is faithful to his covenant promises and that they could live with the life of God's spirit. Given that, they mostly did not attempt to show that every individual thing that happens in God's world happens for the best, and God must have needed it to happen. There is no shadow of an attempt to show that Judas' betrayal was in the end a

---

34 Heb 10:5-7.

good thing, nor Jesus' scourging, nor the preference of the crowd for the release of Barabbas, nor Pilate's political weakness, nor any of these: they were no more and no less than the result of the fact that Jesus was religiously and politically threatening to all kinds of powerful interests. Their statements that the Messiah 'had to' die are not intended as an expression of some kind of fatalism, or as an assertion that God *required* Jesus' death. There is no trace of the view that Jesus' ministry to persuade his hearers to repent and to accept the Kingdom was a charade which Jesus knew before he started was not the real point at all. To say that the Messiah 'had to' die was a standard way of expressing their belief that his death was not incompatible with their belief in the fidelity of God and their realisation that those who stand for the truth – whether Jesus or his disciples – typically have to pay a price for so doing. There is an interesting and highly significant passage in Luke's Gospel, where Jesus comments on two tragedies:

> At that very time were some present who told him about the Galileans whose blood Pilate had mingled with their sacrifices. He asked them, 'Do you think that because these Galileans suffered in this way they were worse sinners than all other Galileans? No, I tell you; but unless you repent you will all perish as they did. Or those eighteen who were killed when the tower in Siloam fell on them: do you think they were worse offenders than all the others living in Jerusalem? No, I tell you; but unless you repent you will all perish, just as they did.'[35]

The context in Luke's Gospel is Jesus' attempt to convey the urgency of his message; but what he here flatly refuses to do is to interpret

---

35 Lk 13:1-5.

every tragedy as somehow a punishment inflicted by God upon sinners or upon a people who did not wholeheartedly listen to Jesus' words. Tragic deaths coming so suddenly and without warning might serve as a wake-up call for us; but that is no justification for the massacre, and no reason to interpret the collapse of the tower as somehow engineered by God to reveal his justice or whatever. These things happen, whether through malice, incompetence or accident, and that's all there is to be said about them. And what is true of those two tragedies can be said also about Jesus' own death. As such, it had no deeper meaning. What was important was that unto death, even death on the cross, Jesus was faithful to what he had been sent to do.

CHAPTER EIGHT

WARNINGS AND EXCESSES

A.   THE WARNINGS

The attempt to provide theodicies – arguments to show that every single disaster or suffering is in the long term a good thing – will be likely to fail. The less ambitious project consists simply in trying to show that even in a world like ours, with its chequered history of human sin, it need not be intellectually dishonest to believe in a good God.

I have been arguing that for the most part the writers of the Christian Bible have in fact been content with what is a theological equivalent of the less ambitious project. That project refused to try to show how each event in the world could be seen to work out for the best. Even in the best of all possible worlds, it need not be the case that every individual event or state of affairs makes the world better than it would otherwise have been. Jesus' death was not in itself a good thing; but it became inevitable, given the political circumstances in which his ministry was set. The Christians learned to see that his fidelity to his mission fitted into the tragic pattern of many earlier prophets, even though in Jesus there was more than a prophet; and to mourn his death as a tragedy without despairing, not because they believed that it had been planned by God, but because they knew it was not the end of the story. God in Jesus was vindicated despite, rather than because of, what was done to him.

The point needs to made with some care, however. For, if we look just at what they say about the event of Jesus' death, it is true that they are grateful for it, regard it as part and parcel of the whole process of salvation: 'Jesus died for our sins and rose for our justification.' But it seems to me that even in this case they are not saying that the death of Jesus was in itself a good thing, or that it was somehow *necessary* for our salvation. Nor do they represent Jesus' death as in itself desired by God, or as the only thing which could have induced God to forgive us. What they do instead is express gratitude and even astonishment that God would reveal himself to us by coming to share life in our world, sufferings and all. In that act of solidarity they find encouragement for their belief that we shall also share in the resurrection of Jesus. Their attitude is that just as, given the attitude of his hearers to religion and to politics, Jesus had to face death if he were to continue to preach what he knew to be the truth, so it may well be that Christians too will have to suffer for their faith: 'The servant is not greater than his master.' But the fact that one might have to suffer in a good cause does not render that suffering a good thing, and it is perverse to suggest that it does.

What I wish to do in this section is to look at some biblical warnings against trying to adopt the more ambitious project in response to The Problem. I shall briefly consider the books called Qoheleth, 4 Ezra and, in rather more detail, the Book of Job. I shall then consider what I shall argue are the unfortunate excesses into which some later Christian writers have been led because they ignored these sensible warnings.

i)   Qoheleth[1]

'Vanity of vanities, says the Teacher, vanity of vanities, all is vanity.' The famous and dramatic beginning to the book expresses a complete mistrust of trying to make any kind of sense of our world, our lives or our history. All is 'vanity', a waste of breath.[2] 'There is

---

1   'Qoheleth' is the title given to the speaker in the book, and 'Ecclesiastes' ('Preacher' or 'Teacher') is an attempt to translate it into Greek. Hence 'Eccles', the conventional abbreviation for references to this book.

2   The Hebrew word being used here is sometimes associated with talk of breath or of breeze. The general idea is that trying to make sense of things is a waste of time, pursuing a will o' the wisp, not going to get one anywhere.

nothing new under the sun.' We are caught in an endless cycle devoid as far as we can see of any ultimate meaning. To lend authority to this thought, it is put into the mouth of a King of Israel who set himself to discover wisdom: the writer probably has Solomon in mind. But even the wisdom of Solomon can conclude only that 'it is an unhappy business that God has given to human beings to be busy with.'[3]

> I have seen the business that God has given to everyone to be busy with. He has made everything suitable for its time, moreover he has put a sense of past and future into their minds, yet they cannot find out what God has done from the beginning to the end. I know there is nothing better for them than to be happy and enjoy themselves as long as they live; also that it is God's gift that all should eat, drink, and take pleasure in all their toil …
>
> … I saw all the oppressions that are practised under the sun. Look, the tears of the oppressed – with no one to comfort them! On the side of their oppressors there was power – with no one to comfort them. And I thought the dead, who have already died, more fortunate than the living who are still alive. But better than both is the one who has not yet been and has not seen the evil deeds that are done under the sun.[4]

Qoheleth is convinced that no sense can be made of any of it. The best one can do is to live as best one can, to seek what happiness is available and not to inquire after any deeper meaning to life. In particular,

---

3   Eccles 1:13.
4   Eccles 3:10-13, 4:1-3.

I saw all the work of God, that no one can find out
what is happening under the sun. However much they
may toil in seeking, they will not find it out; even
though those who are wise claim to know, they cannot
find it out.

The same fate comes to all, to the righteous and to the
wicked, to the good and the evil, to the clean and the
unclean, to those who sacrifice and to those who do
not sacrifice ... This is an evil in all that happens under
the sun, that the same fate comes to everyone.
Moreover, the hearts of all are full of evil, and madness
is in their hearts while they live, and after they go to
the dead. But whoever is joined with all the living has
hope, for a living dog is better than a dead lion.[5]

It would be harder to imagine any bleaker attitude to the miseries
and apparent pointlessness of life. Qoheleth's advice to seek
whatever happiness one can devise and enjoy it while one may seems
almost to deepen the gloom. Yet, so astonishingly that some
commentators have wondered whether the final chapter has been
tacked on by someone else, Qoheleth himself concludes with this
advice:

The end of the matter: all has been heard. Fear God,
keep his commandments, for this is the whole duty of
everyone. For God will bring every deed into
judgement, including every secret thing, whether good
or evil.[6]

Qoheleth seems almost to have been seriously depressive. At the very
least he could not be accused of any facile optimism! But it is

5   Eccles 8:17, 9:2-4.
6   Eccles 12:13-14.

important to ask what, even disregarding the final sentence, one might make of views like his being included in the Bible. The main thrust of his argument is that it is quite pointless to ask questions about the meaning of the universe — not on any large scale, and not even about the meaning of a human life. He asserts that God has made sure that we will not be able to get anywhere along those lines. Yet even this remark need not be understood as being bitter; for the thrust of the book as a whole is resigned, rather than bitter or resentful. Nor does Qoheleth say that there is no point to doing anything. On the contrary, the policy he recommends is to do the best one can to be happy and enjoy life; he is not being cynical; he is simply being realistic and as constructive as he can be in the circumstances as he read them.[7] Qoheleth's own religious belief as expressed in the last couple of verses of his book need not be in any sense insincere, and it certainly is not without important content. For this, he implies, we do know: that God is moral and requires us to be so and that in the end God will judge us with justice.

ii)   Job

The Book of Job probably consists of an original short morally edifying story, into which a long series of largely poetical reflections on The Problem of Evil has been inserted. The short story is of the righteous Job: Satan tries to prove that he only happens to be God-fearing at the moment because his life has gone smoothly; however, Satan suggests, if God permits him to be afflicted, his righteousness will be short-lived. Accordingly Job is afflicted with many sufferings and bereavements. At this point even his wife suggests he should simply curse God and die. But Job refuses:

> Shall we receive good at the hand of God and shall we
> not receive evil? In all this Job did not sin with his lips.[8]

---

7   Eccles 8:15.
8   Job 2:10.

The little story has a happy ending: 'The Lord restored the fortunes of Job', giving him twice what he had had before. It is a simple edifying tale of fidelity in adversity with an appropriately happy ending, which also ends the Book of Job as we have it.

But the writer of the book presumably thought that this pious little tale was too naively simple. So he inserts what is the heart of the book as it is now: a debate no less than forty chapters long in which Job, far from being quietly undisturbed and long-suffering, bitterly bemoans his fate. Yet he still refuses to accept his friends' efforts to help him by explaining to him the true reason for his sufferings. His friends offer what I have called theodicies – attempts to show how God is perfectly justified in treating Job as he does. Job rejects all these theories as either false or blasphemous or both. And right at the end of the long debate, just before the original 'happy ending', the author has God say this to Eliphaz, the first of Job's friends:

> My wrath is kindled against you and against your two
> friends, for you have not spoken of me what is right, as
> my servant Job has.[9]

In short, God says that theodicies are simply not the answer. They should go and offer sacrifice in penitence for their stupidity in thinking that they could make everything clear; and Job will pray for them. The Lord has heard Job's prayer, for Job now knows and accepts that God's ways are not ours. We all have to accept that our minds are far too limited to try to fathom why God should have wanted to create a world like ours.

So what was wrong with all the theodicies? Here they are, with some comments:

9   Job 42:7-8.

a) God may do as he likes: we cannot complain

Job's wife says bluntly that God can do whatever God wants and Job should simply accept it. She will have none of this pious 'The Lord gave, the Lord has taken away' attitude with which the Job of the original little story accepts his fate; 'Curse God and die!' is her advice.[10] The suggestion is that God's actions might well be simply arbitrary: after all, God has the power, he can give or take, make happy or afflict, just as he chooses. Job flatly, almost brutally, rejects her advice; if we are prepared to be grateful for what God gives us, then we cannot consistently accuse him of arbitrariness even if we cannot understand why he has taken something away from us. In effect, Job insists, he does not have to show why God does everything; all he has to do is not deny his faith that God has created a good world overall; he does not have to accuse God of injustice or anything else: still less to say that God might simply be immoral on the grounds that we cannot understand the justification for what he has done. So far, Job has done little more than echo Qoheleth – for even Qoheleth says more than Job's wife was willing to concede.

Nonetheless, unlike the unshaken Job of the original story, Job is now depicted as thrown almost into despair, 'cursing the day of his birth'. 'Why is light given to one in misery, and life to the bitter in soul who long for death but it does not come?'[11]

b) Job himself has sinned

Eliphaz's first effort at justifying God's conduct towards Job invokes the very traditional Jewish idea: sufferings are divine punishments, so Job must have sinned. He must have deserved it. No human being is wholly innocent before God, and Job ought to admit that this is true of himself, too. But he should comfort himself with the thought that if God chastises him, God will thereby heal him.[12]

10 Job 2:9.
11 Job 3:21-21.
12 Job 4:1–5:27.

Job's reply to this is a deeply felt lament: if he has erred in the sight of God, God should tell him; but since he is not aware of having done so, why does God torment him? It would be better to crush him altogether than to torture him like this. Job claims that the Eliphaz brand of 'comfort' only makes matters worse.[13] The modern equivalent would be the suggestion that any woman who has been raped must somehow have been asking for it and should accept her suffering as a well-deserved punishment. Job has no hesitation in saying that such advice, calling as it does for acknowledgement of one's own complicity when one knows one is innocent, just cruelly compounds the problem. Sadly, though, all too often it is psychologically difficult or even impossible for such victims to reply with Job's determination. Bad theodicies are not just wrong, they are often deeply damaging.

c)   *Someone must have sinned*
Bildad, the second friend, insists that even if Job personally is innocent, God's justice simply would not permit suffering and punishment to come unless some sin had been committed by someone. 'Does God pervert justice?' he rhetorically asks.[14] So, he cheerfully continues, if Job has not sinned, perhaps his children have? *Someone* must have, and that is why Job is being punished. Just such a contention is sometimes offered to victims of the AIDS pandemic – even when they are children, or when they are completely innocent wives of husbands who have become infected. That does not stop people from invoking some theory of divine punishment, dreadful as the implications of such a theory almost always are.

Job, however, ignores the suggestion that he is being punished for someone else's sin, and repeats that he is not aware of having transgressed. He admits that nobody is going to be able to stand up

---

13   Job 6:14-30.
14   8:3-4.

in court and prove himself innocent if God wishes to accuse him. He says bitterly,

> Though I am blameless he would prove me perverse.
> I am blameless; I do not know myself, I loathe my life.
> It is all one: therefore I say,
> He destroys both the blameless and the wicked.

And in the same vein

> Are your days like the days of mortals, or your years
> like human years
> that you seek out my iniquity and search for my sin
> although you know that I am not guilty,
> and there is no one to deliver me out of your hand?[15]

Has God so much time on his hands that he has nothing better to do but scrape around looking for sins that are too small for us to spot? Job wonders why, if God had so low an opinion of him, he allowed him to be born in the first place. But in his misery he has half accepted that God does blight even the innocent; for this terrible conclusion stems directly from Bildad's assumption. Contemporary versions of this type of theodicy can have equally disastrous results.

d)   Perhaps Job sinned unknowingly?
Zophar, the third friend, is clear that God is not vindictive and arbitrary, so sin there must have been, even if Job honestly knows nothing about it.[16] Zophar also shifts the suggestion from immorality on Job's part to some kind of ritual impurity – perhaps

---

15 Job 9:20-22, 10:5-7.
16 Job 11:1-20.

because it was easier to forget one of the tiny rules of the Law where ritual matters were concerned. Job dismisses this speculation: it is all very well for someone comfortably off to develop such theories, but Job knows that God is not like that. And Zophar is doing wrong in so far as he is simply lying to protect God's reputation. He is as bad as a quack doctor; the remedy sounds fine, but is in fact quite worthless.[17] Sooner than go along with it, Job will speak up for himself and will demand that God show him what wrong he has done. Will a life after death restore justice for Job? Alas, he does not think so.[18]

e)   *Job is blaspheming in speaking this way*
Who does Job think he is, claiming to know how things are between human beings and God? God will surely strike him down.[19] Eliphaz, who has evidently learnt nothing from what has been said so far, repeats that all suffering is a punishment for sin. Anyone who questions this will perish at God's hands.

Job once more rejects the accusation of ungodliness, despite the misery to which God has brought him. But why do even his friends – his 'miserable comforters' – pursue him, as God is doing? Why is he so completely abandoned? Yet surely, he dares to hope, there will be someone who will speak for him? Surely he will in the end see God?[20]

Zophar and Bildad, unimpressed, return to elaborate at length on the fate of sinners, abandoned and tortured by God.[21] But Job too persists: it is just obvious that the wicked prosper, unavenged, and that innocents like himself suffer for no intelligible reason. To his friends, this is the most shocking of all Job's assertions, since it completely undermines the moral order of the universe as they

17   Job 13:7-12.
18   Job 14:1-22.
19   Job ch. 15.
20   Job ch. 16.
21   Job 18–20.

understand it, an order in which God's justice is made clear.[22] Nothing daunted, Job gives a detailed defence of his own conduct; he has done nothing wrong.[23]

f)   Suffering might be a divine pedagogy

A new critic, not one of the original three friends, now loses his temper with Job's quibbling. He has a new slant on suffering. It is not punishment; rather it is a kind of loving admonition from God which reminds us to repent and improve our lives.[24]

g)   God's final reply

After all this, God does not offer a single word of explanation or justification; he merely reiterates that Job is in no position at all to estimate the worth of the world or to complain about what God might or might not do to organise it better. Job simply cannot grasp such matters, has no standpoint from which he might either question or seek to understand. Job accepts that he has no knowledge of such matters, and has spoken in ignorance. God's purposes cannot be withstood, but are too wonderful for Job to comprehend.[25] Job's final remark is shrouded in ambiguity, but perhaps he repents of having been so bitter in his complaints.

The Book of Job as a whole both expresses the anguish of those who suffer and yet refuses to accept any of the easy and logically neat explanations as to why this is so. These, as Job says, are either simply untrue (for Job is truly innocent) or do not fit the facts (for the innocent do suffer and the evil do prosper) or are insulting to God (implying that he is vindictive enough to punish anyone, innocent or guilty, for human frailty). Surely this should serve as a warning to all theologians not to try to tie everything up too neatly? Job's

22 Job ch. 21.
23 Job ch. 31.
24 Job 33:16, 36:9-12.
25 Job 42:1-3.

comforters claim to understand the ways of God when they do not: as a result, they glibly misrepresent their experience of the real world in order to make it fit their theories. In consequence they are led into claiming that God will punish some innocent person – almost any innocent person – because other guilty person(s) have sinned. Job demands that whatever we say about God has to present God as morally reasonable and, in the last analysis, we should be humble enough to see that it is better to say nothing at all than to present God as arbitrary, unjust, uncaring or vindictive.

iii)   2 Esdras[26]

In some ways this book contains lessons for the reader which are not dissimilar to what might be learned from Job. The book may be contemporaneous with or slightly later than the Christian Gospels, and was certainly known to some later Christian writers. It contains seven visions which the prophet Ezra had, in which he agonised over the fate of Jerusalem, and the destruction of the Jerusalem Temple (in 70 CE).[27] These events, in Ezra's mind, called in question everything about God's relationship to the people with whom he had sworn an everlasting covenant. Meditating on them forced the prophet to try to find some way of solving The Problem of Evil as it had affected him and his people.

In his visions he begins by having conversations with the archangel Uriel (who represents God), in which he tries desperately to understand how God could have permitted such disasters. Ezra knows that evil is in the hearts of every human being since Adam himself; just so, Israel has indeed been unfaithful; but surely Israel has not been more unfaithful than any other nation, and in particular

26 The names of the books are confusing. The book here called 2 Esdras (following New RSV) is also referred to as 4 Ezra; it is among the Apocrypha in both Roman Catholic and Protestant Bibles.

27 The dramatic setting of the book is in the much earlier exile of the Jews to Babylon, and the destruction of the Temple at that time. But the writer is in fact using that experience to comment on the present disaster.

no less faithful than the Babylonians to whom God has now subjected them? How then can God treat his chosen people so much worse than he treats the gentiles? Ezra is bewildered at God's behaviour, partly also because, if human beings have any propensity to sin, that propensity has been implanted in them by God. So God must share at last some of the blame when humans go wrong. The angel, apart from trying to throw Ezra off by some insoluble riddles to show how little Ezra understands ('Measure for me a measure of wind, or bring back for me a day that is past')[28] takes a very unhelpful line: Ezra is simply incapable of understanding the ways of God, and in any event many of the things Ezra wants to know will be revealed only after the end times have come. In a second and a third vision, Ezra complains that it appears as if only a very few people will be blessed after the end times have come, while very many will be damned. The angel replies that God rejoices so much over the saved that he is not concerned with those who are not.[29] Ezra cannot understand why God bothered to create people who he knew would be damned, nor why the just cannot pray that the unjust might be shown mercy by a merciful God. He is baffled.

But then the prophet has a completely different and utterly disorienting vision in which he sees a young woman bemoaning her fate; she had been barren for many years, despite praying for a son, but at long last a son was granted her. Yet this delight too was illusory, for tragedy struck again: on his wedding night the son himself suddenly died. The woman was totally disconsolate and went back to the city. Ezra saw that she was not alone: they were all in deep mourning for the city of Zion, the mother of them all, now left empty and desolate. Indeed the whole earth is mourning for most of her children who are lost without hope. But, surprisingly, Ezra then suggests to the woman that she should still try to acknowledge that

28 2 Esdras 4:5; These are presented as ridiculous, since Ezra feels he is being fobbed off, as indeed he is.
29 2 Esdras 8:37.

God is just in his ways – perhaps then he will even give her back her son. She refuses and Ezra goes on to list the woes of the holy city: the Temple destroyed, the ark of the covenant plundered, the people enslaved, the virgins and wives ravished and defiled. 'Therefore shake off your great sadness and lay aside your many sorrows, so that the mighty one may be merciful to you again, and the Most High may give you rest from your troubles.' Why should she complain just about her personal woe, when the entire city lies desolate? Ezra's vision then takes a terrifying turn, as the woman is thrown to the ground, screaming, and suddenly disappears altogether. But then, in her place, Ezra sees spread before him the renewed and glittering city of Zion in all its glory. The vision ends.[30]

Commentators point out that the only comfort for Ezra himself, and the only comfort he can offer others in his despoiled city, is that they should all renew their faith in the goodness and fidelity of God and pray for the restoration of Zion. As one commentator remarking on Ezra's anger perceptively puts it:

> On the face of it, it is anger over her lack of a sense of proportion, of her exaggeration of personal mourning when all of Zion mourned; below the surface, the anger surely reflects his own desperate struggle, in spite of all, to handle his own distress and mourning.
>
> Once he can offer comfort, he is given comfort himself. The revelation of the future or heavenly city and the experience of it are the true comfort for his grief over Zion's fall.[31]

That could sum up the message of Job, 2 Esdras and much of the Christian Bible. The miseries with which we are confronted in so many ways and at so many levels are such that we are totally unable

---

30 2 Esdras 10:1-46.
31 M.E. Stone, *Fourth Ezra*, Hermeneia Commentaries, Augsburg Fortress Press, Minneapolis, 1990, pp. 321, 336.

to find any individual justifications for them. The efforts people make to try to do so are simply not believable: on the contrary, they are glib, often blasphemous by implication and can easily lead to despair rather than consolation. It is enough to be able to believe in the goodness of God and to trust in that.

B.   SOME EXCESSES

Several eminent Christian theologians to a greater or lesser extent ignored these warnings. The story of later theological tradition is largely a story of metaphors taken out of their traditional settings, taken literally and getting completely out of hand.

Take for instance the notion of redemption. Etymologically, for what that is worth, it means 'buying back'. One can literally redeem slaves from captivity or objects from the pawnbrokers; one can even redeem air-mile coupons by using them to buy back the travel permissions to which they entitle one. Of course, 'redeem' can be used metaphorically as well. A player can redeem a poor first-half performance by scoring a spectacular goal late in the game. In this case, however, the metaphor involved is dead: one does not at all have to think of slaves or pawnbrokers in order to illuminate what one means when saying that someone can redeem their past mistakes.

Then consider sacrifice. Etymologically, the word comes from 'to make something holy', and was employed in its literal sense to describe the way in which things were made holy for God by being put beyond human use: animals were killed, offerings burned. Here too, however, the term can be used in a much wider metaphorical sense to describe the act of foregoing something of value for the sake of achieving something else. People have sacrificed their careers to save their marriage, or their marriages to further their careers; parents will make sacrifices for their children. But obviously in these uses there need be no reference to God or of dedicating things to God, still less to killing animals. Our modern western sense of 'sacrifice' has no such implications.

Is God to Blame?

In trying to make religious sense of Jesus' violent and shameful death, the Christian biblical writers sought for concepts taken from their own religious tradition which they could use to think of Jesus' death as useful in the eyes of God and good for us. They could readily find instances of killing for God's sake – Jewish tradition was rich in various kinds of sacrifices: animals were killed to express a covenant commitment; the Passover lamb was killed as a symbol of gratitude to God, other animals were sacrificed to purify a person in the eyes of God, or to take away sins. So the death of Jesus the Messiah was therefore very naturally described as him sacrificing his life for us. To think in this way enabled Christians to make sense of what he had done, occasionally in terms of the traditional sin offering, more often as liberating them from the anger of God just as the Passover lamb liberated the Jews from Egypt, or as establishing a new covenant in Jesus' blood. I have argued, however, that despite this emphasis in much of Jewish tradition the principal focus of most of the New Testament writers simply was not on the value of his death as such, but on the sacrifice which Jesus' obedience to the Father eventually required of him.

The early Jewish Christians almost certainly did not think that Jesus was a redeemer in the literal sense of someone who pays a ransom. The various words which they used in this connection were just as commonly used in the extended sense which is typical of dead metaphors, and meant simply the removal of any unwanted restraint. In general, though, when the New Testament writers talk about Jesus redeeming us by his blood they use the terms within a living tradition; they lived in cultures where animals were literally killed in sacrifice and people were literally bought out of slavery. It was natural for them to think of the violent death of the Messiah in those terms, and the possibility of interpreting both of them literally in the case of Christ was always available to them. Nonetheless, I incline to think that for Christian biblical writers the words for redemption express dead metaphors most of the time, and perhaps all the time.

In any event, the difficulties arise when these terms are developed in detail, understood literally, and used in a culture where their literal application is either non-existent or shocking or both. This is just what happened in the case of these two metaphors. In their attempts to show that God was justified in permitting even the death of his Son, the notion of redemption was developed in detail.

A literal analysis of redemption requires at least the following features:

i) A state of subjection

ii) Someone who is powerful enough to keep someone else in that state

iii) The recognition that that person has some rights to maintain the state; or else that the person has the power to insist on conditions required for the release of his hostage/slave.

iv) The money or other consideration required to obtain release.

Later Christian writers set out to show how these requirements for the use of 'redeem' were satisfied in a totally literal sense. Human beings were held in subjection to sin, not just in a metaphorical sense, but literally held in the power of the devil and his evil spirits; the devil was in a position to insist on a price being paid for their release; and the price he demanded, and God agreed to pay, was the death of the Messiah. Hence St Irenaeus writes:

> The mighty Word and true Man reasonably redeeming us by His blood, gave Himself as a ransom for those who had been brought into bondage. And since the Apostasy unjustly ruled over us, and, whereas we belonged by nature to God Almighty, alienated us against nature and made us his own disciples, the Word of God, being mighty in all things, and failing not in His justice, dealt justly even with the Apostasy itself, buying back from it the things which were His own.[32]

32 Irenaeus To Combat Heresies, V, i.

Origen elaborates on this approach: Christ offered his body to God as a sacrifice, and gave his soul and blood to the devil as a ransom payment. But the devil in trying to exercise his power or rights over Jesus had overstepped the mark; and eventually realised that he had been deceived when the dead Jesus was raised to life. In Origen's view, however, Jesus was not offered *in our place*, but offered himself as our representative.

Similarly St Augustine:

> Men were held captive under the devil and served the demons, but they were redeemed from captivity, for they could be put up for sale. The Redeemer came, and paid the price; He poured forth his blood and bought the whole world. Do you ask what He bought? See what He gave, and find what He bought. The blood of Christ is the price. How much is it worth? What but the whole world? What but all nations?[33]

> The Redeemer came and the deceiver was overcome. What did our Redeemer do to our Captor? In payment for us He set the trap, His Cross, with His blood for bait. The Devil could indeed shed that blood; but he deserved not to drink it. By shedding the blood of One who was not his debtor, he was forced to release his debtors.[34]

Anselm's position is set out in the form of a dialogue in a treatise whose title consists of exactly the right question: *Cur Deus Homo? — Why did God become Man?* This classic of early scholastic theology has, as it seems to me, one extremely good feature, but also one which seems to me less than happy. The good feature is that Anselm refuses to interpret the notion of redemption literally and seeks to

33 Commentary on Psalm 95, n. 5.
34 Sermon. cxxx, part 2.

reinterpret it using ideas which were current in his own culture rather than in the Mediterranean culture in which Jews and Christians originally wrote. So instead of insisting on these notions being taken literally and interpreted in terms of payment, ransom, death, blood and suffering, Anselm interprets them in terms of the honour properly due to a feudal Lord from his vassals. Honour violated demands that honour be restored, the debt of honour satisfied. If the Lord simply forgot about the insult to his honour, he would be behaving unjustly by making no distinction between innocent and guilty vassals; and forgiving without satisfaction is a violation of the proper order of human relationships. God could therefore not simply forgive our sins without satisfaction being made; and because of the infinite nature of any violation of the honour of God, no satisfaction that any sinner could make would suffice. Anything we could do, by way of repentance, penance or revision of life, would have us do no more than what is now our duty, but obviously this would not at all compensate for the dishonour given to God in the past. What is needed is a human being who can make an infinitely valuable satisfaction on our behalf. And that is why God became incarnate in Jesus. God, for our own good and in the light of his own dignity, could demand no less.

Anselm clearly wishes to avoid invoking anything like a literal use of sacrifice or redemption. He nowhere suggests that God demanded the sufferings or the death of Jesus; what he asked for was the obedience due to a Lord. If living out this obedience to God involved Jesus suffering and being put to death, that was a brute fact of history, but not a necessary condition of our salvation, contrary to the impression many of his Christian predecessors had mistakenly drawn from the Bible.

What I believe is less happy about this account is that Anselm still wishes to work with some notion of a debt to be paid, even if it is now a debt of honour; and Anselm believes that it would have been contrary to God's justice simply to have forgiven us our sins freely and without any penalty at all.

Abelard disagreed with some of the details of Anselm's account; but more seriously, he denied that even the weaker Anselmian notion of a God demanding satisfaction was at all appropriate, or even consistent with everything else Christians would want to believe. Like Anselm, Abelard also rejects the literal use of the term 'redemption'. He argued that if the devil has power over us, it is because God has permitted it; but certainly the devil cannot be said to have any rights over us, however much we may have sinned. And if there is no sense in which a ransom is due to anyone – there is no question of anyone having to make some kind of payment to release us all from an alien power – must we not call into question the very notion of making satisfaction even as Anselm understood it? Moreover, is it not just a mistake to say that it would have been morally outrageous had God or Jesus simply decided to forgive us? Is not such forgiveness with no strings attached exactly what the Lord's prayer requires of us all? And if it had been necessary to make enormous repayment for our sins, how much more should we have had to pay for crucifying God's son? The entire metaphor has got out of hand. A God who demanded satisfaction and set such a high price on his honour is simply not the God Jesus preached.

There has recently been some extremely important discussion in Northern Ireland seeking the best way to bring about harmony between the two communities. It has taken the South African Truth and Reconciliation Commission into consideration and tried to learn from that experience in applying it to their own context. There are many serious questions to be resolved: should there be an amnesty for even the most dreadful of past actions, not so as to forget them, but to forgive them? And is simply to forgive those who seek forgiveness without asking any more from them somehow a betrayal of justice, or is it rather a wonderful way of showing that even justice may not always be the most important virtue which we are called upon to practice? Abelard's question 'Could not God simply forgive?' is a very live issue even for us. As we have already seen, there may be two issues intertwined: what we should ask of ourselves in such circumstances and whether we are right to expect more of God than we would ever expect of one another.

Abelard's own view seems to me to have been very close to that of Paul and John. In revealing to us the loving dedication in obedience of the Son to the Father, Jesus enables us to accept the gift of his love in ourselves, so that we too can live as Jesus did.

Sadly, Bernard of Clairvaux sharply criticised this view on the grounds that it amounted to a denial of the objective character of the redemption, replacing 'genuine' redemption with the mere idea that Jesus set us a very good example. Abelard's book was condemned before he had a chance even to explain his position to his critics.

He was, however, fundamentally right. Aquinas later conceded the key point, that there was no need for Jesus to die in order for our sins to be forgiven.

> Even this justice depends on the Divine will, requiring satisfaction for sin from the human race. But if He had willed to free man from sin without any satisfaction, He would not have acted against justice. For a judge, while preserving justice, cannot pardon fault without penalty, if he must visit fault committed against another – for instance, against another man, or against the State, or any Prince in higher authority. But God has no one higher than Himself, for He is the sovereign and common good of the whole universe. Consequently, if He forgives sin, which has the formality of fault in that it is committed against Himself, He wrongs no one: just as anyone else, overlooking a personal trespass without satisfaction acts mercifully and not unjustly. And so David exclaimed when he sought mercy: 'To Thee only have I sinned' as if to say: 'Thou canst pardon me without injustice.' [35]

35 Rom chapters 9–11, especially the final conclusion in 11:32-36.

This is the key point, because if Jesus did not have to die, then there is no need to try to show why God should have thought Jesus' death a good thing. Many medieval theologians, including Aquinas himself, did persist in this attempt. In so doing they still perhaps think that these terms somehow have to be kept and understood in some literal sense, just because biblical writers and later Christians did use the language of sacrifice, satisfaction and redemption. Anselm saw that he did not have to accept this imagery in order to understand what Jesus did for us. It is entirely permissible to say that Jesus died because his ministry seemed religiously suspect to influential Jews and politically unhelpful to Pilate (who took care to keep Herod onside). This is intelligible, unedifying and, sadly, in a world like ours, not in the least astonishing. Jesus' death can readily be explained. In that sense, the sufferings of Jesus as such have no more religious significance than the sufferings which many millions of other human beings have had to face and are still facing. What is significant about Jesus is his teaching and his unshakeable faithfulness to his vocation and to the truth; and what shows that he was more than yet another political martyr is that he rose from the dead. That is the truth on which all the Christian biblical writers insisted, and the context in which Jesus' and our sufferings need to be seen.

Part III

CHAPTER NINE

WHY HAVE YOU FORSAKEN ME?

The problem which most exercises us is surely in the first instance a problem about personal suffering and pain. At the level at which it makes its impact, it is not going to be 'solved' by philosophical and theological theorising; nor indeed by theories about pastoral counselling. Nevertheless, the theoretical background against which we live our lives, explicit or implicit as it may be, can make a great difference to the ways in which we try to cope with suffering and pain. If the foregoing chapters are at all along the right lines, they will have highlighted that one aspect of the problem is the need somehow to understand. There is a deep-seated instinct that suffering can be better borne if we can see some meaning in it, some ultimate point which makes bearing it in the long run worthwhile. In an ordinary everyday way this need can sometimes readily be satisfied. We can understand that the pain attendant upon a visit to the dentist or a serious operation has a point; we can see how it is an unavoidable part of the process of restoring our health. We can understand why we have to endure the more boring aspects of our jobs or the more irritating behaviour of our adolescent children, and we can devise strategies to cope with such burdens and for seeing them as part of a positive picture. The pay-off is well worth the pain. 'No pain, no gain', we can even manage to say, though sometimes through gritted teeth.

The problem becomes altogether more serious when we are faced with sufferings which have no visible point to them. Sometimes these are deeply personal, for instance a bereavement or a debilitating illness; sometimes they are on an almost cosmic scale – a Holocaust, an earthquake, a tsunami, a vicious genocide lasting for decades, endemic poverty and deprivation. The need to find a point, a meaning, in such situations in order somehow to cope or make sense of our lives and our world is really desperate. I have argued that on this cosmic canvas such a need, desperate as it is, in the end cannot be met. We have only a very limited and modest understanding of human motivation and human malice, only a very incomplete grasp of the complexity of the natural world and little or no grasp of the point and value of the Universe as a whole. It is not that questions such as, 'Why?' and 'How?' and 'What is the point of it all?' are out of place, least of all when we find our lives blighted or degraded. Up to a point, of course, some things can be explained: tsunamis are caused by the movement of tectonic plates, AIDS by the mutation of a virus, genocide by hatred, jealousy and greed in a situation of limited resources. Jesus, like many another, was killed for perfectly understandable reasons. But these explanations, perfectly true as they are, are not remotely at the level we wish them to be.

I have tried to explain why explanations at the highest level are beyond us and why this need not in itself make our religious beliefs dishonest or superficial. I have argued, and more strongly, that attempts to meet the need for cosmic explanations are likely to do more harm than good. Consider the types of theodicy which have been, so to speak, on offer and consider how in the light of them one would then speak to a woman whose infant child has just died. There is absolutely no moral or theological justification for trying to offer anything remotely like the following theodicies:

i) Somehow God must be punishing you, perhaps to lead you to repentance
ii) The child's death and your suffering are part of the satisfaction God requires in order to redeem fallen humanity's unfaithfulness. We live in a fallen world and must take the consequences

iii) God is sending you this trial to test your faith

iv) You will be a stronger and better person for having managed to cope with this terrible event.

Explanations like these are just what some – and not just a few – believers feel they have to offer. But surely 'comfort' along these lines is precisely what the book of Job considers blasphemous. The first involves an immoral theory of vicarious punishment which renders theism totally disreputable. The second, perhaps slightly better for being less personally vindictive, is still an attempt to take some biblical language as intended literally where at least in the Christian writers it is usually intended in no such way – and on those occasions on which it is intended literally, it makes sense of any kind only in a culture in which the sacrifice of living animals, even human animals, might be thought of as a praiseworthy religious act. And indeed only recently there have been what are thought to be ritual religious killings of infants whose decapitated bodies have been found, for example, in the Thames in London; so such things must presumably make some sense to some people even in our own day. Yet despite the fact that the overwhelming majority of people in our culture would regard such conduct with uncomprehending horror, when they articulate their Christian faith many well-meaning people will still insist on interpreting the death of Jesus along very similar lines, and must therefore have somewhere in their minds a picture of God which is ultimately equally horrific. I have argued that the motivation for such enormities can be traced to our very understandable need to find ultimate cosmic explanations when we are in no position to find them because at that level they simply are beyond our understanding. There are absolutely no good grounds for suggesting that such blasphemy must somehow be at the root of Christianity.

The third and fourth types of explanation are perhaps less misdirected than the first two. They do contain at least an important grain of truth, in that religious faith can be strengthened by being clung to even in the face of the most dreadful suffering; and suffering can make people stronger in themselves and so perhaps more ready to sympathise with others. Maybe that is why people can still find consolation in Keats' description of the world as a 'vale of soul-making'. But there are serious problems even with these suggestions.

First, although it is true that suffering can have positive effects in this kind of way, it is certainly not true that it always does; and neither is it true that people, even if they want to, always have the psychological resources to choose to grow in strength and moral maturity through their sufferings. Sufferings can be totally overwhelming, can make people seriously ill and can often enough break their spirit entirely.

The second problem is the casual acceptance of the idea that God will deliberately set up such situations. In Christian terms, did God intend the preaching of Jesus to fail to convert his hearers, as it largely did? Did God as it were set up the crucifixion from the start? Of course, as things worked out Jesus was able to give an example of courage under oppression, an example which has inspired millions of people. And even though it is true that God knew 'in advance', so to speak, that in a world such as ours the good are likely to suffer, he did not know in advance – merely in virtue of creating such a world – in what way, if at all, that generalisation about human nature would play out in the life of Jesus.

Towards the end of his life Jesus began to see very clearly what the probable consequences of his preaching would be. In his last few hours this realisation terrified him. The first three Gospels make no attempt to hide this fact when they recount Jesus' prayer in Gethsemane just before his arrest. The Gospel of John, in a more detached and theological manner rather than by narrating that event, makes a similar point, though it does not present Jesus as being in agony.[1] Notice, though, that Jesus does not seek any cosmic

---

1   Mk 14:33-37.

explanation for his forthcoming sufferings. He does not even consider any of the 'theodicies' just mentioned. What he does is pray that events may prove him wrong and that things will not come to that. What he commits himself to is a fidelity to his ministry. In showing us how a human in such extreme desolation ideally should respond, Jesus gives an uncompromising commitment to be faithful to his truth, since that is the mission his Father had entrusted to him. He prays as he recommended that all his disciples should pray: not, if possible, to be put to the final test, but that God's will be done.

The Gospels differ in the ways they seek to present both the event and the significance of the crucifixion and death of Jesus. Matthew and Mark both present Jesus as utterly alone: his disciples had fled, and even the women who loved him could look on only from a distance. Matthew in particular shows no signs of depicting the dying Jesus as other than mocked, derided and in the end feeling totally abandoned.[2] None of Jesus' friends or disciples even appear in Luke's description of Calvary; but in describing Jesus' conversation with the thieves crucified with him, Luke notes how Jesus exemplifies another part of the Lord's prayer: he offers God's forgiveness; and Jesus' last words are of resignation and a hope that is very far from despair.[3] None of these three evangelists make any attempt at all to answer Jesus' agonised question, 'My God, why have you abandoned me?' Neither do they in any way suggest that it should not even have been asked. It is exactly the question which humans in any extremity naturally feel is so urgent for them; the need for understanding is all the more desperate because no answer can be had other than the ordinary this-world answers: he was perceived as a political threat or as religiously unwelcome.

In this respect, the Gospels' attitude to Jesus is very similar to the way in which the Book of Job deals with the character of Job. The Job of the original pious tale is too simple, too neat to reveal the

2   Mk 15:40, Mt 27:55.
3   Lk 23:42-46.

agonising nature of some human suffering. What the writer of the book does with this narrative is to re-write it in the darkest and yet most realistic of human terms: the questions are real, obvious, natural and desperate; it is the cheap answers which simply will not do. We have to learn to live with that uncomfortable gap. Luke's answer lies not in explanation, but in hope: not in saying what a good thing it really was (from some mysterious point of view which we cannot grasp) that Jesus was betrayed, suffered and died, but in emphasising that even those horrors cannot in the end separate us from the love of God. 'Father, into thy hands I commend my spirit.' As is not infrequently the case, Luke on this point is very close to Paul:

> Likewise the Spirit helps us in our weakness; for we do not know how to pray as we ought, but that very Spirit intercedes with sighs too deep for words. And God, who searches the human heart, knows what is the mind of the Spirit because the Spirit intercedes for the Saints according to the will of God.
>
> We know that all things work together for good for those who love God, who are called according to his purpose. For those whom he foreknew he also predestined to be conformed to the image of his Son, in order that he might be the first-born within a large family. And those whom he predestined he also called; and those whom he called he also justified; and those whom he justified he also glorified. What then shall we say about these things? If God is for us, who is against us? He did not withhold his own son, but gave him up for all of us, will he not with him also give us everything else?
>
> … Who will separate us from the love of Christ? Shall hardship, or distress, or persecution or famine or nakedness, or peril or sword? As it is written

> For your sake we are being killed all day long
> We are accounted as sheep to be slaughtered
> No, in all these things we are more than conquerors through him who loved us. For I am convinced that neither death, nor life, nor angels, nor rulers, nor things present, nor things to come, nor powers, nor height, nor depth not anything else in all creation will be able to separate us from the love of God in Christ Jesus our Lord.[4]

This paragraph is not an expression of some simple vague optimism. It represents a very careful synthesis of the various arguments Paul has so far deployed in this letter; and it leads into his final argument that God is far from abandoning his people in Israel, no matter what they have done. Indeed Paul's arguments here strongly suggest that he believed that in the end all human beings will be saved.[5] For all that, in human terms all we can do in such extremities is to recognise that we no longer know how to address God; we have no adequate prayer on our lips. When the victim of the Holocaust said, 'Where was God? Why was he silent?' and Jesus said, 'Why have you forsaken me?' these were not prayers in any comfortable sense, nor even were they petitions. Yet Paul insists that the Spirit of God remains with us even in such distress, and is the motivation for all our prayer even when we have no words of our own other than those of abandonment. It is precisely because the risen Jesus himself shared in our sufferings that we too can have confidence that we will share in his life. The presence of the Spirit in us even now is the guarantee of that promise. Given that belief, nothing can ultimately separate us from God.

Paul's is a theological argument, addressed by a believer to fellow believers in danger of persecution. To what extent does it represent a

---

4   Rom 8:26-39, citing Ps 44.
5   Rom chapters 9–11, especially the final conclusion in 11:32-36.

means of comforting the afflicted? In my own view, it does not directly provide comfort at all, and would be cheapened were it to be used in such a way as to suggest that it does. The best way to comfort the afflicted and those suffering agonies is not to tell them that it will be all right in the end, as though that was an answer to their deepest questions about why God permits *this* and where is God *now*. It is not an answer to those questions at all and should not be presented as if it were. The Problem of Evil is not the same as the problem of suffering. The problem presented to us by suffering is how to cope with it, how we can live and relate to others when our mind is so preoccupied, our emotions so deeply engaged, our whole being in torment. In such straits, what we need is courage, support and perhaps above all patience. Sometimes what is most constructive for those in desperate suffering is for others to help them not to repress how they feel; and perhaps that is best done through empathy and compassion. When all that can be done to alleviate the pain has been done, we need personal support, not argument. What we certainly do not need, and what is unfortunately so often offered, is bad arguments to explain why this suffering is ultimately a good thing, when it so obviously is not.

That being said, these Pauline texts and the Christian Bible in general do point to a dimension in human experience which need not be destroyed by any such sufferings, and that is the presence in us of the Spirit, the Risen Jesus with whose life we live. That awareness of God in the depth of ourselves is not on the same level as the joys or the disasters of a human life. It is an awareness of a dimension of our experience which is not in that way 'practical' at all. To have learned to be in touch with this gift of God is not to have learned 'the solution' to The Problem of Evil. Rather it is to have the lived experience that nothing need separate us from that gift; and to hope that that realisation will be there for us at all times, come what may. The place for thinking about The Problem of Evil, ideally at least, is when one has time to reflect upon one's religious faith and to try to reconcile it with those features of the contemporary world which seem to threaten to make any such belief impossible. I have argued that this can be done in all intellectual honesty. Unfortunately, however, The Problem is apt to feel at its most pressing when we are in real difficulty and leisured thought is a luxury beyond our reach. But like Job we can even then refuse to flirt with theodicies which are false and even positively harmful. Even when one might feel abandoned by God, one can still with honesty commend oneself into the hands of God in faith and in hope.

DESCRIBING GOD

It is easy to see that our ideas about what God can and cannot do are intimately bound up with what we believe we can truly say about God. It is equally easy to see that to describe God is going to strain our language, and hence our minds, to their utmost limits. Our experience of things is bound up with the structure of our own consciousness, and that in turn is intimately related to our senses and to our physical constitution generally. We have trouble describing anything which is not directly and immediately the kind of thing which we can sense. We typically use two types of strategy to cope with this limitation as best we can.

The first is to use descriptions in which our words are given a sense which is 'stretched' beyond the way in which they are used in more everyday descriptions. Think of the meaning of 'attract' in saying that two people are attracted to one another, and that the earth and the sun are attracted to one another by the force of gravity; or 'memory' used in connection with ourselves and of a computer. Or the many ways in which 'exist' is used, to speak of the objects on my desk, colours, fictional characters, numbers and moments of time; and, one should add, 'exists' as used of God, who is not an individual thing or property at all. God's love for us is not a psychophysical state as is our love for one another; yet we want to use the same word, albeit in its 'stretched' sense because of the kind of connection we believe we can discern between the various sense of words we use in this way.

The second is to use words in their straightforward everyday sense, to refer to something we wish to use as providing an illuminating comparison. 'We have a mountain to climb if we are going to solve this problem', 'That is money down the drain', 'He is a couch potato', 'a butterfly mind' and so on. All the words in those expressions have their ordinary meanings; but in using them as a basis for what we take to be helpful comparisons we are not describing things straightforwardly. We are describing metaphorically, asserting that a particular comparison will help to understand whatever it is we are trying to describe. In such descriptions the words have their usual senses; it is the description as a whole which is to be understood differently.

Metaphors, however, are by no means trivial 'optional extras' in our attempts to describe the world. Scientists must frequently have recourse to metaphors to describe events or entities which are beyond our direct experience. They urge us to think of the origin of the universe as a big bang or a collapsed star as a black hole, space-time as warped or the ultimate constituents of reality as tiny strings vibrating in ten dimensions. These are all attempts to make the usefulness of a particular theoretical mathematical model into something which we can in some way grasp. The metaphors are to be taken seriously, but not literally. In much the same spirit, God can be said to have walked with Adam in the garden, an image of a level of intimacy which has an immediacy and simplicity which would be hard to duplicate. I am not, of course, suggesting an unlimited hospitality to metaphors, whether about God or about anything else. Metaphorical statements which simply do not help to give any insight will either be meaningless or downright false. For example, I think it meaningless to say, however metaphorically, that my best friend is a bowling green – I have no idea at all how to understand such a comparison; on the other hand, I would think it false rather than meaningless to describe him as a hippopotamus, because I can imagine people whom I could perhaps truly describe in that way, though happily my friend is not one of them.

The general point is that there are activities that only a physical being can literally perform, yet, since our experience is embedded in our physical world, it is hard for us to describe anything outside that world other than in metaphorical terms. To speak of God as speaking to us, or hearing us, are metaphors, not literal truths, but they are nonetheless true precisely in so far as they are helpful – since they do convey something of the reality of God. If we ask what God can and cannot do, we need first of all to be careful to be clear in which sense a proposed action is being described. Can God hear? Of course God can. ('God hears us' is, let us suppose, a helpful and therefore true way of describing part of our experience.) But of course 'God hears' understood literally is just false. That, and many other such things, are things which God literally cannot do.